Starting Over

Chronicles of a Self-Reliant Woman

Jackie Clay

ISBN 0-9718445-9-3
Copyright 2004-2008

Backwoods Home Magazine
PO Box 712
Gold Beach, Oregon 97444
www.backwoodshome.com

Edited by Ilene Duffy, Rhoda Denning, and Lisa Nourse

Introduction

Six months into their journey to start a new homestead in the Minnesota wilderness, Jackie Clay's husband, Bob, died. Widowed with a 14-year-old son and caring for elderly parents, Jackie Clay never thought about giving up. She was determined to build her new home in the wilderness.

But Jackie Clay is no ordinary woman. She has inspired thousands of readers with her articles in *Backwoods Home Magazine* with her perseverance, homesteading knowledge, and wisdom. By her side is her son, David, who becomes a man as this remarkable story unfolds.

This is a wonderful journey that still continues today. Come step into Jackie Clay's world with the thousands of others who watch this modern day pioneer carve a home in the wilderness.

Chapter One

$\mathcal{W}$olf tracks the size of my hand came right up our path to the creek, to within 200 feet of our campsite on our new homestead in the north-woods of Minnesota. I was alone this morning, early…just a little after dawn's pink "can see" had barely arrived. An inch of new snow had fallen during the night, but the ground was warm yet and the spring temperature was above 40°. I glanced around to see where the tracks led. Was our visitor standing in the bush, watching me? Feeling a primal thrill, I slowly turned to study the trail of tracks. This was what we were here for. The wolves, moose, deer, and hundreds of miles of big woods. I was a bit disappointed; the wolf tracks zigzagged over the rise we would be building our home on and meandered down to the spruce and balsam along the beaver pond below.

I greeted the warm full sun as it slowly crowned the pine-covered far-away ridges, then walked back to the tiny camp that would be our home until we had our larger cabin built. It felt good to relax. The sale of our Montana homestead and the 1200-mile move in midwinter had been exhausting at best.

Our camp was a combination of a 32-foot travel trailer and an 8 x 12-foot fish house. We would be living in it until we had built the first part of our new house.

Our camp had been chosen carefully beforehand. For two years we had known that our lovely homestead in Montana would be but a stopping place on our quest for a "wilderness forever" home for our family. (Perhaps you remember me telling you about our try for a great, very remote piece of wilderness in northern British Columbia and the heartache we faced when Canadian Immigration closed the border prior to Y2K and would not let us in.) So we settled for a comfortable piece of Montana mountain "almost wilderness" instead. We did the best we could at the time. But now we had found our real home in the north-woods of Minnesota.

Roughing it with an old travel trailer

We knew we would be buying raw wilderness land and needed a little better camp than tenting afforded. So we looked around and finally got a huge deal on a travel trailer. The words "fixer-upper" were stretched when we began working on the $600 trailer. It had leaked for years, and the paneling and floor was rotten in several spots. About everything that could freeze had frozen and split. Cupboard doors hung off hinges and insulation hung from the ceiling. But it had potential and we got to work remodeling it to fit our needs.

A travel trailer is not meant for remote use or winter use in cold

Trailer and shack are united! We have a home.

climates. Where that is tried, the plumbing quickly freezes, which is what had happened in our new "old" trailer. And plumbing includes the toilet holding tank, full of not-nice stuff, frozen solid. We did not know when our place would sell and wanted the trailer winter-ready. Just in case, we weren't planning on using the water system.

So we tore out all inside paneling and some of the two-inch wall studs and rafters which had rotted from constant leaking. Then we spent weeks ripping out rotted insulation (including mouse nests and living families of mice) and bagged it up. Cautious about hantavirus, which is carried by white-footed deer mice, the inhabitants of our trailer, we wore face masks and frequently washed up with soapy water while doing this work. (Hantavirus is contagious to humans and has caused deaths each year.)

Then, using a 12-volt power driver, we screwed in new structural members, added new insulation, and replaced the paneling.

Likewise, we tore out cupboards, replaced doors and shelves, evicted more deer mice, replaced flooring, built new shelves in the kitchen to accommodate our lifestyle of large tins full of dry goods and lots of pots and pans, and fixed the bathtub and surround. (We knew we wouldn't be using the water system, but could use a battery operated solar shower in the tub.)

Slowly, our beater of a trailer became our home-to-be. And, to make it truly "home," as I knew it would be for months, I took the time to decorate it in our northwoods style. Using moose as a theme, I glued wooden and rusty tin little moose cutouts on the cupboards, made moose curtains, found forest green curtains at the dump, and put moose towel racks here and there to hold loose items. Cabin fever is a very real thing and when three people step down from a spacious thousand-square-foot home, I did not want our tiny trailer to seem a prison.

Then we set about beginning to stock the trailer with permanent camping supplies, from long underwear to dry food housed in tins to keep our mouse buddies from wanting to repopulate their former abode.

In Montana, while we were waiting to sell, we used the trailer as a grab-and-git unit, just in case one of the numerous forest fires forced us to evacuate. One can never be too prepared. It would be better than escaping with the clothes on our backs and would put us in a much more comfortable position than having to camp on the high school gym floor until the fire was out. We saw hundreds of people doing just that during years of fire seasons and didn't want to join their ranks.

The shack

After our trailer was ready, we planned to build an 8 x 12-foot "porch" or "shack" addition to be temporarily attached to the trailer through a sort of insulated air lock. This would afford us more elbow room and allow us to safely hook up my wood kitchen range, along with a small propane wall heater.

My oldest son, the innovative Bill Spaulding, found an insulated 8 x 12-foot fish house on a trailer frame and wheels for sale for about what we would have had invested in lumber and materials for the same "shack" that we had planned to build.

So we camped at Bill and Kelly's Minnesota home and gutted the fish house, getting it ready to remodel to suit our needs. (With five holes cut in the floor, it looked like a huge outhouse.) It was not a thing of beauty, with white foam insulation and dead ladybugs and flies suspended from the ceiling by plastic film. But it was a building we didn't have to build, and we were glad to have it.

After two days, the weather

The shack is finished, complete with a $9 ceiling fan with light.

moderated a bit, and we decided to move our large travel trailer north. But could we get in? Our realtor in Cook told us that the seller had offered to try to plow a trail in to be neighborly. No matter that he lives 40-some miles away. But northern Minnesota is known for its great people. As added insurance, Bill hooked his snowplow onto the front of his big Ford truck and, early in the morning, we headed north leaving the small livestock comfortably stabled in the enclosed stock trailer.

Plowing out

We made it up only to find Ross, the seller, plowing hard but making little headway in the three-feet-plus of hard granular snow. In two hours, he'd made perhaps 100 feet, with better than $^8/_{10}$ of a mile left to go. Not good. For a few minutes my heart sank to my stomach. Were we nuts or something?

We didn't mind being snowed in, once we were in, but we sure couldn't drag the trailer in over three feet of snow.

Then a miracle happened. A great young man named Josh stopped by, obviously seeing our problem and said he had a high-track Cat bulldozer on a trailer, and he could go home and get it if we wanted. He'd have to charge us $250 to plow in, but we figured it would be money well spent.

Josh returned with the huge dozer and started shoving a hole in the snow. But darkness threatened, as the days were very short in February, and he had no lights. We followed him in Bill's pickup truck, trying to give him enough light to see by. (Of course it didn't help that he'd never been up the trail he was plowing.)

But he made great progress, and in a short time he had plowed all the way in to our land and opened up a large campsite and two landings, one near the road to park vehicles when we would be snowed in, and another down in the woods. Thank you Josh.

As soon as he had left, Bill began "tidying up" the plow job with his snowplow, widening and cleaning the trail nicely. By nine o'clock we hauled in the trailer and set it into place. I was so grateful I nearly cried.

11

Now if we could only get the fish house up and set into place, and the livestock trailer in before it snowed badly again.

Talk about your cliff hangers. It seemed like we'd been holding our breath about something or another for months. Would it snow three more feet? Would the existing snow blow the driveway shut?

Finally, the day came when we could haul the fish house up north. We had lucked out, and only a little snow had fallen in the interim. Bill loaded his tractor on his flatbed trailer, which we pulled with our truck, and northward we went again, and in four hours Bill had the fish house off the trailer and into place next to our travel trailer, with only eight inches between them. I was really impressed. It was snowing, but we were in business.

Joining trailer and shack

We stuffed old camper sofa cushions between the door of the trailer and the hole we had sawed in the wall of the shack so that we could access both shack and trailer. There was sort of a very short hallway between, stuffed on all sides with the old cushions to keep out the bitter cold until we could sheet it up with plywood.

We soon had our animals at the camp with us, except the horses which we boarded at a neighboring farm with the propane wall heater hooked up on the shack's wall. Bill left us with the temperature hovering around zero, hoping we wouldn't freeze solid overnight. I'll admit that the travel trailer, which had been unheated all winter, was like winter camping outside in a snowbank. No, I've camped in much warmer snowbanks.

David claimed the old sofa in the shack, right in front of the wall heater. Smart boy! And we piled bedding on deep. It was cold, but the next day, having had heat on for the night, the trailer warmed up. But the dog water pail still had ice on it all day.

I knew Bill had worried about us, because he called at eight o'clock that morning to see if we were still alive.

The "necessities"

Now, when you move to a bare homestead in the middle of the winter, you cannot dig an outhouse hole. Nor can you use a travel trailer for anything else than a tent with solid walls. With these challenges, we were forced to get creative. There was a toilet in the trailer bathroom, so I lined it with a plastic, biodegradable kitchen trash bag and dropped a handful of cedar animal bedding into the bottom. This took care of our solid waste. Every time you use the toilet, you throw the toilet paper into a lined waste basket and cover the waste with a handful of cedar chips. Liquid is handled by using a three gallon pail, which is rinsed and dumped in the woods daily.

When full, the solid waste bag is topped off with more chips, and tied shut. These are stacked carefully in a metal barrel, waiting for the ground to thaw so the whole works can be buried in a safe location. (I recently opened one of the older bags and was happy to note that there was nothing but brownish black compost in the bag, not vile stinky, disgusting you-know-what.) This will make a great fertilizer under some newly planted trees.

Water

Other necessities of life are difficult to come by when you move to a naked northern homestead with no buildings in midwinter. Water first comes to mind. We've melted snow before, but this snow had melted and then frozen, making three feet plus deep piles of rock-hard white stuff instead of nice fluffy snow. (I must admit that the first day here our goats drank five dollars worth of bottled water.)

But that couldn't go on, not on our budget. One thing I've learned in life is that when you need something, ask around. Even if you're really, really new in an area. People in rural areas are usually very happy to help out someone with a little initiative and a friendly attitude. We needed a free, good, nearby water source, without inconveniencing anyone. At zero and below, all stores' and gas stations' water faucets are turned off for the winter.

The first person I asked was a wonderfully friendly older lady who drives a school bus in Cook and also works part-time at the local *Subway* shop. And we hit the jackpot. "Sure," she smiled, "you can get water at the big spring at Idington, right on your way home." Then drawing directions on a

The tired old enclosed stock trailer that got our animals here and became a temporary goat and sheep barn. We have wolves and coyotes for neighbors.

napkin, she went back to work, but only after inviting us to attend her church when we got settled in.

So off home we went, via Idington, a settlement south of Cook so small that you don't even know when you're in it. But off on a dirt side road was a sparkling spring, flowing two-inches of crystal water out of a plastic pipe in the snowbank. It was such a gorgeous site to our worried eyes. Our water needs were temporarily met. When the snow melted, we'd have plenty of animal, garden, and bath water from our own stream. And, hopefully, come next winter, we should have a well drilled by hand at our garden site.

It's funny; I read somewhere that when you must hand carry water, a household uses something like 10 gallons of water a day. Then when you get a hand pump, it goes up to 20 gallons. Add running water and a flush toilet and the amount goes up to something like 200 gallons per day. We used about 15 gallons a day, and that washed us and our dishes, gave drinking water to the house, five large dogs, five goats, and two sheep.

I could have used more water. I do like to soak in a 25-gallon bath to ease a sore back, but a stove-heated solar shower, hung in the bathtub, has to do for now. And I had to wash clothes in town, which I hate. Recently I found a wringer washer in two pieces at the dump. With a new cord, it works great and I am happily saving $40 a week. Then with the warm weather, we are again able to haul 100-gallons-plus of water from the spring in white plastic 55-gallon barrels on the pickup.

School

David enrolled in the Cook School when we were settled in. Cook is a town of 622, or so the sign says. But they have a large school, including a swimming pool and cafeteria. Our kid is a country kid to the bone, and his last school in Craig, Montana had nine children in the entire school. So Cook was culture shock for him. He'd never ridden a school bus nor eaten hot lunch in a cafeteria. Or been with so many other kids. But he's a brave soul and gets along well with nearly everyone, so off he went on the big yellow bus. (It did help because he gets to ride a snowmobile or ATV to the end of our trail, a mile from home, where he catches the bus.)

Mom bought us a set of handheld two-way radios for Christmas, which were invaluable on our trip cross-country. They were put into use again as David rode out to catch the bus and then back in the afternoon. We have bears, wolves, and moose in the area, but our biggest worry was that he'd have mechanical trouble. Which he did. Several times. A gas leak drained five gallons of gas overnight. The U-joint of the ATV wore out and left him stranded. But a call on the two-way brought Mom or Dad in the pickup truck in five minutes.

He calls us when he is getting on the bus, and again when he gets off the bus. It takes him about 10 minutes or less to drive home. So if he's delayed and doesn't show up we go out looking for him. We only had to do that twice, and both times while we were getting the system down. He'd simply forgotten to call.

We've got a lot of work to do on our new homestead. Luckily, we did move here in February, because it will give us all summer to do the work that must be done before we are ready for winter. In Minnesota, you constantly think of things that you need to get ready for before next winter.

Protecting our stock

We had twin projects pop up just as the snow melted. These were a good pasture for our three horses and a barn for our goats and sheep. The very wolf tracks that thrilled us on morning walks also made us very conscious of the peril our small stock would be in, not protected from predators—especially at night when the big boys came out to hunt.

At first we housed our small livestock in our enclosed 16-foot stock trailer. That took the pressure off that project while we lined up fencing for the horses. The ground was still frozen, but in the middle of spring we were able to drive steel T posts into the soil. As we were not able to dig to set our corner braces, we resorted to Mickey Mouse corners to get us by until we could. On two corners, we were able to use existing trees. Another let us tie into a large, high, solid stump. But on the last corner, we were forced to sink T posts on past the corner to act as anchors, or deadmen, so we could stretch the wire and still leave room for the wood corner post and brace posts.

The one side we could not fence lay along the creek and 10-acre beaver pond. The water is deep and we don't think the horses will swim it. But just to be sure, we strung heavy gauge electric wire out, tree to tree, in the water. Having been fenced in Montana with a solar electric fencer, the boys are very used to a hot wire and stay strictly

The crew moves in before the barn is finished, but they're all happy.

16

away from anything that looks like an electric fence. To string this wire, we used our canoe. I'll bet not many people have done fencing on their homesteads in a canoe.

Just as soon as the horses were secure in their pasture, we set about seeding in 10 acres of alsike clover on the other side of the knoll our campsite rests on. As clover grows very well up here in the northland, we decided a better pasture would be a help. Using a whirly, handheld seeder, we spent a day walking over rotted logs, around stumps, and through light brush, overseeding the clover among the native grasses. I would have rather have plowed and disced the ground, but due to logging on the land, this is impossible at this time. In a few years, the branches and

David strings horse fence from a canoe!

logs will have rotted, the stumps turned to mush, and we'll make a pretty pasture.

With the spring rains, the clover sprouted very well, indeed, and we now have little two-inch alsike clover plants sitting cheerfully under the shelter of brome and orchard grass. With this and our other new pasture, the horses will have more than enough forage for the entire year. Later on, we will plow one of the cleared pastures and seed it to grasses and clover to be cut for hay for the animals.

The nightly howling of nearby wolves and coyotes spurred us on to get to work on a goat barn. The arrival of two sets of goat twins also turned our thoughts to a larger goat and sheep shelter than our tiny (it now seemed) 16 x 6-foot stock trailer. But our tiny shelter also needed work, as it was far from weather-tight and pretty.

The goat barn

So we split our time between the shack and starting a goat barn. We decided on a 12 x 20-foot goat barn, which would allow two roomy goat pens, a milking stanchion, and room for David to park the ATV during cold or rainy weather. Goats can make do in smaller quarters, but in Minnesota small livestock spends most of the winter inside as the snow gets too deep and temperatures are too low for them to venture out much. We also needed a kidding pen for the mama goats and their young.

As the ground was still frozen, except the top layer, we chose to build the goat barn on a railroad tie foundation, instead of making a pole type barn. The first step was to whack the brush off in the area we had chosen. This area was fairly flat to begin with, sat on a little knoll with good drainage, and was next to a down-sloping hill with lots of brush, grass, and small poplar trees—a goat's heaven. This will be their pasture. It is near the house site, and we will be able to keep an eye on them and bring them inside every night for added protection from predators.

After David whacked the brush on the site (his favorite job), we further rough-leveled the ground and bought 10 railroad ties. They are already creosoted for protection against rot and dampness.

Being careful to square and level the building, we carefully chose the best railroad ties, laid them end to end, cut to length where necessary and left an opening six feet wide for the center doors and aisle. Much minor leveling was needed, digging out rocks and building up small irregularities in the ground.

We had bought a large trailer load of assorted lumber that a friend had gotten while buying a shed full of firewood at an auction. After he loaded his firewood, he found that the lumber was hidden underneath. But, having no use for it, he sold the whole load to us for $60. One-inch boards, studs, and assorted two-inch planks were ours.

Then we found 22 nail-ridden 4 x 8-foot sheets of wafer board at the dump on two days' visits. Our goat barn was up and running.

We framed the walls on the ground, using 16-inch-on-center for the measurement of the stud spacing. Our sill plate and top plate were cut long enough to span the gaps where the railroad ties joined each other so that the plates strengthened the framework. Spiking the sill plates to the railroad ties, we also allowed enough overhang that the sheets of OSB (wafer board) hung down five inches on each railroad tie. In this way, we could also securely nail the OSB to the ties, further strengthening the construction. The barn is built on a knoll which receives quite a bit of wind due to previous logging, and we did not want it to fly away.

The fish shack

When we were rained or snowed out, or were just plain tired of working on the goat barn, we tackled making our "barn" more homey. Buying three sheets of drywall (on sale, of course), we spent a day sheeting up the ceiling. Not only did this look much better, covering up the hanging insulation, plastic, and dead insects, but it held in precious heat. I really hate taping and spreading sheet rock compound, but in such a small building, even that went quickly. I did the first coat, including all the screw dimples, in one morning.

The next afternoon, I sanded everything smooth, noting how much the compound had receded as it dried. Yep, it really did need at least two coats like the directions said. So I got out the drywall mud and hit it again, using a wide knife to draw it as smooth as possible, reducing the sanding that was inevitable.

I had a gallon of white primer and slapped a coat on the next day, but it was too white. In such a small room, I really needed light, but toned down so it didn't scream. So I dug in my savings box, pulled out a $10 bill, and headed for town. The next day, I slapped two coats of light tan eggshell semigloss paint on the ceiling, varnished two rough 2 x 6-inch planks and topped off the new gorgeous ceiling with rustic "beams."

It looked so great that I also stained many 1 x 4-inch boards to match, using them for trim on the not-so-nice wood grained paneling that had been on the walls of the fish house. Not bad. Not bad, at all.

Adding a strip of wall paper border around the top that was a pine/woodsy motif and a few sets of deer antlers, and our little shack had magically been transformed into a tiny backwoods cabin. The whole project took all of three days, working part-time, as we continued to work on the goat barn.

As the goat population had grown, we had to get the mama goats out of the trailer. The ewe Shetland sheep had given birth to a tiny lamb. We needed to protect all these young ones, so a move to the unfinished barn became a necessity. We slapped up two roomy pens under the partially roofed goat barn, and we were in business. They were protected from the elements as well as predators, and had more room and privacy. Just about what our little cabin afforded us. ⌘

Chapter Two

Spring breakup had finished here in northern Minnesota, and the remnants of huge snowbanks poured rivers of melting water onto the mile-long trail as the warm April sun beat down. Having been only a logging road used during the winter, there were puddles big enough to float our canoe, so our first priority was to do some heavy duty road work with old-fashioned equipment. A couple of shovels, a hoe, and a pick completed our manual tools. The good old four-wheeler worked to haul trailer load after trailer load of rock and gravel into the worst clay holes.

Repairing the road

We had done remote road work a lot before this in the mountains of Montana. There, too, we lived a long, long way from a maintained road.

We have learned a lot and still have much to learn about keeping roads driveable with little pocket cash. First of all, we worked hard to drain off any water standing or running onto the road. There is usually a higher side to a trail and a lower side. The trick is to channel the water down onto the lower side, then find a place to trench it off into the woods or a marsh. This was not done once, but many times, as the water in holes lowered, requiring more work to get them as dry as possible. We are still always alert for puddles on the road that need help draining. Our little ditches get plugged up with silt and leaves, and mud from passing vehicles can create a dam, blocking water flow.

Depending on the soil, some wet spots need only draining and fill. Others, with clay or muck bottoms, need large rocks for a bed, then loads of gravel on top of the rocks to raise the roadbed. Water will not stand on higher ground. Only low spots will retain water, no matter how long it rains.

Our son, David, loves to do road work. (Don't we all like to create little channels and watch water flowing?) He dug and filled many low spots, channeling the water off at every opportunity. It gave him an excuse to run the ATV and do road building at the same time. We were still leaving our Suburban out near the road and running in gas, feed, supplies, and spring water with the four-wheeler to avoid tearing ruts into our soft road. Once you make huge ruts, they are with you for a long time. And they get worse and worse. We really didn't mind the so-called isolation and inconvenience of not driving in and out. And slowly the road got drier and the worst holes became more solid.

We learned to create a "poor man's culvert," too. In several spots, the original trail builders had used a backhoe to dig fill out of one side of the trail and build it up. Unfortunately, in several spots, they picked the uphill side of the trail. During snow melt or heavy rains, these little ponds fill up and seep out onto the trail. Working for two days, we dug out a little dip about two feet wide and a foot deep to the downhill side. Now, this drained the pond pretty well, but it would also tear up our vehicles when we drove the trail. Not to mention what the propane truck driver would say. So we lined the ditch with fist-sized round rocks. This let the water flow through, but gave the vehicles a good bed to drive over, with little bumping to deal with.

Our road building really picked up when my oldest son, Bill, was finished with his tractor the first of May and told us to come on down and pick it up for the summer. Glory be! That Ford tractor has a gravel bucket that holds three times as much gravel as David's little trailer does. And it scoops it up, too. We also picked up Bill's cement mixer to begin our footings and foundation on the new house.

It was an exciting time, watching the leaves and blooms come out on the trees, berry bushes, and wild flowers, knowing that we were finally getting ready to really get to work on our new homestead.

Our poor goat barn was only about half done, but it held the critters well out of reach of predators. In the daytime, they ranged about happily grazing and browsing on grass, tree leaves, and brush. At night, they were shut in their pens. But we had to leave it undone, in order to get on with other projects. If there is one thing I've learned: you can only do so many things in a day's work. Period. You may want to do this or that so badly that you can taste it. You wake up at night trying to figure out how to work more. But the fact is you can do what you can do. No more.

Spring was great. We had four goat kids born from two does, four long-eared, wonderfully spotted, cuter-than-heck, silky bundles of bounce. I traded off the first two for some sheeting for the goat barn, giving us a milking doe and a gallon of goat milk a day for the house. I could hardly wait to make yogurt, cheese, and ice cream again. The second set of twins I left on the doe, who also milked a good gallon of sweet milk. I wanted to keep the doe kid and I didn't want to be milking two does with everything else I had to do.

We needed to get a garden started, the road improved, and get our house under way. Winter comes too quickly on spring's heels in the North. With the tractor, the house site was easily leveled. First I scraped the top foot of good topsoil off to one side, digging out all the tree stumps I could. This left only two solid pine stumps, which would end up under the house in the crawl space, but out of the way. The benefits were that I didn't have to work for many days, and taking the stumps out would have left a soft spot near the footing that might weaken the foundation. It seemed the best option.

All of the other rock and gravel was sorted as best as I could. Any that seemed fine enough for cement went around the outside of our site to be used when we mixed the cement. The large rocks went in another pile, as we were going to use those in the foundation, using slip forms and stacking the nice round granite rocks artistically. The rough, in-between gravel was hauled out onto the worst holes in our trail. There are advantages to building on a gravel ridge.

Most days, I averaged about eight loads on the road a day and much of that time was spent in travel. It would have been nice to have a dump truck, but we didn't. Then there were chores, cooking, house chores, and water hauling. The days went by fast. Too fast.

Putting in the gardens

When I got tired of hauling gravel, we hacked at the new garden spots. I had trays of tomato plants in the window of the fish house that I started back in late March. They were lusty and large by the end of April, begging to go out into the soil in their cozy Wallo' Water tipis. So we worked hard at getting the new garden roughed in.

Now, some folks figure that because we've been homesteading for decades that everything just naturally comes easier for us. Sigh. Sometimes I wish it were so. Unfortunately, we have to work just as hard to accomplish most things as the next person. And, no, we don't have perfect, fluffy black garden soil, either. I feel somewhat like Jackie Appleseed, having carved innumerable gardens out of clay, rock, and tree roots, only to move onward in the quest for a better homestead that we owed less money for.

Whacking brush in the new garden. Surprisingly, the Troy-Bilt tiller turned under some fearsome brush.

Here, as we began working on the garden, we decided on two garden spots. One, on the slope downhill from our building site, had beautiful soil and faced the south. It was also quite close to the creek and small beaver pond, should we have to pump water on the plants during dry spells. The other was downslope from the goat barn, right smack in the middle of small popple trees and hazelnut brush. But there was the possibility of tripling the size of this garden in the following years, due to the lay of the land. This site also faced south and east.

While we worked, our tomatoes grew.

So the small spot below our future house was tilled and made into three beds which measured four feet by twenty feet each. And this is the spot we chose for our baby tomato plants. We dug out the rocks, roots, and grass clumps. Blueberry plants were pulled out, brush was dug out and hauled off. It made us feel like murderers pulling up all those lusty blueberry bushes, with their little pink buds, when in the catalogs, the same bushes cost $7.99 and up. But on our land, there are millions of blueberry bushes, and these were, in effect, weeds. And weeds are simply strong growing plants, growing in the wrong place for a person's convenience.

I worked in some lime, as the soil here is acidic, along with some of the rotted manure out of our stock trailer. We worked these beds extremely well, then planted 32 tomato plants of four varieties which I liked in cold climates. These were Early Goliath, Early Cascade, Oregon Spring, and Stupice.

First we laid down red plastic mulch to increase the soil temperature. Then in a few days, we began planting, cutting "X"s in the center of the plastic to receive our plants. After planting each plant very deeply, which grows nice strong roots along the stem, we set a five-gallon plastic bucket down over it, upside down, and placed a Wallo' Water around the bucket to hold the Wallo' Water in place while we filled the cells with water, then we removed the bucket. We had to haul our water to the site in five-gallon water jugs, so we were only able to plant a dozen

25

plants a day, filling each empty tipi with sun-warmed water. Even though the nighttime temperatures dipped into the high teens, our little baby tomatoes took right off in their little individual greenhouses.

We had left enough room on the bottom sides of the beds to plant green beans and wax beans. This area we kept worked up with our handy little Mantis tiller until the danger of frost was past and it was safe to plant these frost-sensitive crops.

While we waited, we worked like mad on the big garden. Big? Ha! The best we could do was an area about 20 by 75 feet. We were right in the brush, and we tilled, hacked, dug, and chopped with axe and grub hoe trying to get out as many runners and roots as we could, fearing the whole garden would pop right back to brush again. Then there were the rocks, logs, stumps, and tree roots. We kept the garden cart and a couple of five-gallon plastic buckets on hand to receive this "trash." The rocks went out onto our trail and the wood went back into the low corner of our horse pasture. My, did we work for that spot for our large garden, even though it was half the size of my smallest garden out of four in Montana. But it was a start and it was all we could do right then.

In this spot, we planted onions, carrots, and radishes, and later on, when it had warmed up, sweet corn, melons, and squash. The weather was warm, and very soon, we had a garden. If only the deer would let it be.

Spending less time in the garden than I had ever done in my life, I turned my focus to the house and resumed hauling gravel and leveling the hillside.

It was about this time that my youngest sister called from Michigan asking me if I would come get my elderly parents, whom she was living near and helping out, so as to give her a break. She had been super stressed with a business, his and her parents, among other things, and needed to breathe.

So we shifted our focus and prepared to have house guests in our little travel trailer and fish house shack. My sister, Sue, who lives in a suburb of Duluth, an hour and a half south of us, and I readied for a trip to Michigan. Right in the middle of the best building weather in Minnesota. But, like I've said, you do what you can do.

My husband, Bob, is a great guy but doesn't have the drive that I do. Okay, so I'm obsessed with getting things done. Can't help it. And David is only 13. So I was not surprised to find the place just as I left it a week later, when I drove into the yard in Mom and Dad's station wagon. Oh well, the animals were happy and the place hadn't burned down.

My son, Bill, had found a loaner oldie travel trailer for us to "camp" in while Mom and Dad were there visiting. Five people and three dogs are just too much for one shack. So I cooked in our old shack and spent the day in and out of there, not wanting to leave Mom and Dad alone, as they both have health issues, including Mom's recent heart attack.

The building site

When the trail was driveable with Mom and Dad's car (it was hard for them to get in and out of our big four-wheel drive vehicles), we finished leveling the building site. We were having trouble getting it right because of the slope both ways, and were very happy to have Bill drive up with a transit on the front seat of his truck.

Like a pro, he set things up and had me hold the pole. We had cut batter boards, which are simply two sturdy wooden stakes with a 1x4,

The batter boards and string to keep things square and level. The inner string has been removed for ease of pouring cement.

*After a 90° day of cement pouring
we are cement spattered and tired.*

about two feet long, screwed to the top. You pound in the stakes outside each corner, making a 90° corner on which to fasten strings to mark the ends and sides of the foundation. We needed two of these for each corner, making eight in all to mark the corners and string all four sides so we could dig footings correctly. I wanted two feet of rock foundation above the footings on the downhill side, so with the transit, we slowly worked the batter boards which were about two feet outside of the actual corners, and strings, which crossed at the actual corners, until things seemed right.

Of course, on measuring, the rectangle was out of square, measuring first the sides and ends, then across the diagonal, making an X. Both sides of the X need to be the same length, and of course, both sides and both ends needed to be correct, as well.

It took most of the afternoon, adjusting the screws which were on top of the 1x4s to wind the strings tightly on, but slowly, our adjustments were minute and the measurements were accurate. When we had the outside four cords nearly perfect, we added the inside set, making the double markings with which to gauge our footing's width.

When we had all the cords stretched tightly, I only had to measure 16 inches down from the strings to the top of the footing trench, which would be the top of the cement, to find level. When we dug, we had a stick with a black mark at one foot and we only had to stick that in our trench to find out if it was deep enough.

We are building on a very firm old rock and gravel point and dug our footings out a foot deep and a foot wide. This we did by hand with a pick, shovel, and pointed hoe. And like our other "waste" from the site, we hauled the not so good stuff out onto the trail, saved the finer gravel for cement work, and sorted out the large rocks to go into the foundation.

And the preliminary work was even more fun because Mom and Dad were there to share it with us. Even though having them entailed more work for us, it was a real treat to have Mom thrill to each new blooming wild flower and to look up from cement work, and to see my 92-year-old father driving the riding lawn mower down the foot path to see how we were doing. After all, they took me away to the woods when I was real little, and frequently all the time I was growing up. It only seemed right to have them there with us while we were starting our wilderness homestead.

Fruit trees

Taking a break from digging the footings, we began to plant the four apple trees that my sister, Sue, and my parents gave me as a pre-birthday present. We had been very short of cash and I had not been able to buy new fruit trees this spring, even though I considered it a near-necessity. So with those great potted trees in the stock trailer (to protect them from the goats), we began to ready a spot for them.

By then, David was using Bill's tractor (with permission, of course), and doing a darned good job, too. Not only was he scraping up gravel and hauling it to the trail, but he had learned to ditch and dig holes with the gravel bucket. So I had him scrape the brush and logs from our new little orchard spot and then dig four widely spaced holes for the trees.

It's best to dig a hole at least twice as big as the root ball of the tree. We did better than that with the tractor. Each tree had a hole four feet long, two feet deep, and three feet wide. And each hole was dug in about 10 minutes. With a shovel, you couldn't have dug half that hole in a whole day.

He tipped the bottom lip of the bucket, which has power down, then drove forward. This caused the bucket to dig in well. As he went forward, he lifted the bucket to level, then raised it when the hole was wide enough. Driving forward a few more feet, he dumped the dirt and repeated the process several more times, each time working deeper and deeper. When we had a good hole, he went back to the yard and got a bucket full of old rotted manure from the stock trailer pile. Then we carried the first young tree to its spot.

When you plant potted trees, you don't want to disturb their roots. So, instead of just dumping the tree out, we carefully cut away the plastic pot with a sharp knife, being careful not to cut the roots too badly. Then, gently, we peeled the plastic away, with the tree in the hole. While one of us held the trunk gently upright, the other shoveled topsoil and gravel into the hole next to the tree. Filling each hole took longer than digging it because we had to do it by hand. We certainly didn't want to risk damaging those trees by using the tractor.

Bob and David free the new apple tree from the pot.

After the tree was planted to the level it had been in the pot, leaving the graft well out of the soil, we wrapped wire screen around the trunk several times. Mice, rabbits, and voles will completely girdle a young tree by eating the tender bark during the winter. So the screening was a must. We applied it right down below the soil so that when we mulched the trees, the rodents couldn't get under the mulch to nibble on the tree. We protected the trees up to three feet, as the snow does get deep here. We were extra happy, as that screen came from the dump out of discarded window screens.

The screen was tied with twine to hold it in place, but not so tightly that it would impair future growth.

After the tree's trunk was protected, we forked a good layer of strawy mulch around it for at least four feet in diameter. Not only would the mulch help hold in moisture during the hot, dry months, but it would prevent any grass or weeds from competing with the young tree and protect it from intense cold during the winter. As a bonus, the manure would slowly feed the little trees into winter and beyond.

We pounded in four six-foot steel fence posts outside the ring of mulch so the goaties and deer couldn't munch on the trees, which they most certainly would. Even moose delight in crunching up tender young fruit trees. So we made a stout fence out of wire stock fencing around each tree as it was planted. We made our circles five feet in diameter. (We should have made them ten feet, as we found creative goats could stand on the wire and nibble leaves, bending over after a rain.)

When the trees were snugly in their little corrals, I went around and tied a soft twine here and there, to help straighten up a couple of tops that were growing a little crooked. Ahhh, almost done.

While I was fastening the twine, David hauled out a big barrel of water and the little gasoline Homelite water pump. We pumped ten gallons of water on each tree, completely flooding the little basin it was rooted in. This helps settle the soil, reducing the possibility of any air pockets around the roots. If it had been dry weather, we would have gently watered in a whole 55-gallon barrel on each tree. But it had been raining and the soil was already moist.

Once a week, unless it had rained well, we watered our new little orchard and delighted in watching the leaves spread out and bask in the spring and summer sun.

Garden pests

In the mornings, even with Mom and Dad to care for now, I enjoyed walking down to my little gardens and watching the plants grow. Now in June, I could see eight long rows of sweet corn four inches high and growing, beans with three sets of leaves, onions reaching for the sun, and tomatoes coming to the top of their snug Wallo' Waters. The gardens were little, but things were really growing well. The good, virgin soil was fertile.

But one morning, the garden didn't look so good. Around each place a corn plant had been was a little hole and although the wilting plant was there, the kernel of corn was gone. As we had no crows yet, we figured the culprits were either chipmunks or ground squirrels, which we have in abundance. And, darn it, we enjoy watching the cheerful little critters. (They kind of remind me of me, the way they pack away food for the winter.) Traps and poison are out. We couldn't fence them out, so I just had to watch as they destroyed all but the last three corn plants. I did find out that they don't relish beans or any other garden crops. So I tilled up the corn plot and planted extra beans. We could always use more beans.

Then I planted six more tomato plants in this "big" garden, as I now had the space for them.

The footings got dug, but we were slow. Part of that was the extra time it took to care for Mom and Dad. And Dad, because of his damaged lungs, needed to participate in a pulmonary rehab twice a week. You can't build a house and drive to town at the same time. But my son Bill told me that if we could get the footings and foundation in and floor it over, he and his friends would come up for a weekend and frame up our little story and a half house for us. I was worried, but comforted.

Then, nearly to the end of my parents' visit, my youngest sister called again and said that if Mom and Dad wanted to, they could stay in Minnesota with us. Again, we were happy to hear this, but the timing stunk. But, then, when is timing right? It would have been easier if we could have gotten the house finished first. Summer was underway, and we were still digging footings.

But finally they were finished, including the two support pillars in the center of the house to support the crossbeams which would stiffen the floor joists.

In each trench, we laid two lengths of steel reinforcing rod to strengthen the cement footings and help prevent cracking. These were supported by laying large rocks at each end and every five feet, all the way around. Where rods were "spliced," the ends were simply overlapped by a foot or so and supported with rocks. We held the rods up six inches from the bottoms of the trenches to get the most strength we could from the rods.

And we began to mix cement. We hauled the water to the site in 55-gallon barrels in the pickup, started the siphon with the water pump, then just folded the hose and stuck it in the back truck pocket when we wanted to shut off the water flow.

Using the handy, clean, on-site gravel, we were able to save time and money. The gravel was a good mixture of coarse sand and rock, so we used a mixture of six shovels of gravel to each shovelful of Portland cement. First we'd pour a little water into the rotating mixer, which worked off our generator hauled to the site. Then gravel was added, then cement and enough water to make a pourable mix.

We found that two batches could be mixed together, and we could still easily handle it in a wheelbarrow. Bob and David mixed cement and hauled it to the trench and I would shovel it into place around the reinforcing rod. Then they would dump the remainder. I was in charge of running the shovel down into the cement to make sure air bubbles and vacant spots were removed, leveling the cement and measuring exactly 16 inches from the top of the cement to the taut string above, run from our batter boards.

We tried to pour at least half a side at a time but the weather did not cooperate. This year we've had a lot of rain. That slowed down our already snail's pace. I do the best that I can. It may not be someone else's best, but it's mine and it'll have to do.

The "free" trailer

About this time, we knew we could not get the house in move-in condition before cold weather hit in October. I was getting unsettled and couldn't sleep at night. There had to be something we could do differently.

Once again, my son, Bill, had the answer. "Why don't you pick up a free older mobile home and have that hauled up? You could use that to camp in for the winter and get at the house in the spring."

Now I absolutely hate everything about mobile homes—except that they are bigger than a travel trailer and it would be instant (or almost instant) housing for the five of us and our pets. I gritted my teeth and told him to see if he could find us one. Mom and Dad were quite happy about the prospect, not having the intense feelings about trailers that I do.

In a few days, Bill called to say that he'd found us a freebie; a 14 by 70-foot, three-bedroom trailer in good shape "for a free trailer." And a fellow that worked near him would haul it up to our land for about $600. "You can shove it way back into the trees," Bill said, "so it won't show later on. You can always use it for storage..."

But that much living space for $600 struck the Scotch in me, and I did feel a sense of impending doom lift from my shoulders. Yes, we could start the house again in the spring. I knew that we couldn't fix up the old trailer and get it ready for winter and keep on working on our new house.

Something I've learned in life is that everything doesn't have to happen when you want it to. Sometimes it just has to wait until later. It's like when you live way remote and plan a trip to town during the winter. You wake up and the storm clouds look ugly over to the West. No use in fighting the way things are. There are other days. It's just how it is in the backwoods. ❧

Chapter Three

Spring had changed to summer, seemingly overnight. The first of the blueberries were already getting ripe and the wild red raspberries hung heavy on their brambles, scattered here and there across the long hill on our new backwoods homestead in northern Minnesota. The goats ran wild across the clearings during the day, constantly snacking on popple twigs, berry tips, and wildflowers. But there was plenty for all of us, and we didn't mind sharing. Our goats and sheep seemed to delight in their new home, almost as much as we did.

But summer in northern Minnesota is way, way too short, especially when you're trying to establish the bare bones for your new homestead, as we are. It didn't help that this past summer was the coldest summer on record in Minnesota history.

I had gotten up early the 26th of July, intent on visiting our two gardens on the edge of the wilderness, which we had hacked out of small openings in the trees. Somehow, just walking among the growing plants that looked so vital and healthy encouraged and uplifted me.

The tomatoes were already two feet tall, having had their cozy Wallo' Water tipis removed two weeks ago. They had plenty of tomatoes set on their vines, some of which were already starting to turn color. The Early Cascade and Oregon Spring tomatoes both set fruit even when the weather is cool, so at least a dozen plants offered fresh tomatoes in a week or less.

We had been running around like the proverbial chickens with their heads cut off last summer, trying to do too many things all at the same time. We were immensely enjoying having Mom and Dad living with us and being able to tap into the vast storehouse of knowledge they have. But with Mom in a wheelchair and Dad able to get around with a cane and helper, I was spending a lot of time doing other things than pouring cement and nailing nails.

I was not frustrated with the caregiving, but with not getting things done I wanted to. After we had finally decided we would get the old, free mobile home that my son, Bill, found for us to use as temporary housing while we built the house, our efforts had switched from finishing our rock foundation to cleaning up the place the mobile would be put when it arrived.

I had been kind of avoiding my tomato beds below the now-abandoned house site, as it was just too depressing. Although I know we'll pick up the construction again in the spring, the home site looks dismal and sad. I'll admit that a few mornings I went out there and sat down and cried.

David gives Grandpa a tour of our new Minnesota homestead

But after giving myself a pep talk on that sunny, clear, cool morning, I set off with our old three-legged Labrador retriever, Pup, to check the garden. All the way out there, I marveled at how well the blueberries looked, hanging heavy with green, luscious fruit, bending the branches down with the bounty. It was going to be a very good blueberry year. And we have about a quarter mile of hillside, covered in blueberries.

When I reached the tomato beds, I stopped stock still, not believing my eyes. Every tomato plant, every pepper, and the rows of bush beans in front of the tomatoes were black and drooping dismally. It had frozen last night. On the 26th of July! Not frosted lightly—frozen. I couldn't breathe for a long minute. The backbone of our garden was gone; perhaps the tomatoes were not dead, but would sprout from the roots, but it would be too late to produce a crop. There was just nothing to do about it.

Two weeks before the killing freeze, my tomatoes were snug in their Wallo' Waters and doing fine.

Unfortunately, gardening is like love. Sometimes it is wonderful, sometimes it smacks you in the face. But if you don't run the risk, you don't find the joy. This disaster totally enforces the reason for keeping at least a year's worth of food on hand. Luckily, I still had boxes and boxes of home canned tomatoes, tomato sauces, salsa, peppers, green beans, and more stacked neatly in our storage building in town. Without this, our loss would have been more of a disaster.

And likewise, it just goes to show you that those folks who laugh at establishing a good garden as a guard against future emergencies, saying if something happens, they'll grow a garden are in for a rude shock. You don't always get a crop when you plant your plants or seeds. A first-year garden is that much more of a gamble as the soil is not enriched and is full of roots, grass, and weeds. I've had more than one garden that took three or four years to hit excellent productivity.

But nothing would have saved our garden this past summer. We had no warning of a freeze. (And who would expect one near the end of July?) I cried a bit and walked home to tell the family.

A used mobile home

But bad times don't last, and a day or so later Bill called to say our not-so-new mobile home would be hauled in a week. Were we ready? Well, pretty much so. I had been cutting the gravel hill down, hauling the excess down the trail, filling in bad spots that we had trouble with during spring breakup.

We had chosen a site for our trailer, about 300 feet from where our new home was to be built, as we didn't want to view the trailer from our new log home. Yet we wanted it fairly close so we could share a water line from the well when that was drilled later on.

Fixing a tractor

David asked if he could haul gravel with the tractor. I hesitated. He had been riding with me on most of the trips and carefully watching me scrape dirt, move piles of old logs, and dig stumps with the bucket of Bill's Ford tractor. I finally let him run the hydraulics, dumping the gravel on the road and start the tractor in the morning. But I told him that he would have to have permission from his older brother to actually run the tractor by himself.

David was nearly 14 and has worked with us and equipment of all sorts since he could handle it, but I would never turn him loose with someone else's equipment without permission. (It helped his cause that Bill had also grown up with farm equipment and had driven tractors since he was about 11.)

I've always stressed safety, safety, and more safety with the kids, and David is no exception. So I caved and asked Bill if he could use the tractor.

"Yeah, sure. If he breaks it, he fixes it," he answered.

So David began learning more about the tractor. First I loaded the bucket and he hauled it down the road to spread. Then he began digging gravel and leveling the trailer site. This freed me to help Bob pick up other roots, lengths of rotten logs, and dig rocks that were in the way.

Actually, it was I who "broke" the tractor, rupturing a hydraulic hose. And, yes, I did fix it. But, boy, was that a chore. That fitting must have been on the tractor since it was built in 1951. We bent a wrench on it and it wouldn't budge. There wasn't room enough to get a large pipe wrench on it. We were stumped.

I called Bill and he suggested getting a map gas torch. A what? It's like a propane torch, but burns much hotter. You know, the yellow tank. Okay. Off we went to town. After a lengthy search, we finally came home with a new hydraulic hose and a map gas torch and tank. We cooked the fitting considerably, and it did finally loosen with another wrench with a pipe slid over the end to lengthen it for extra leverage. If you do this, remember that there is a risk that you could bend or break the wrench. But most times, you will not and the added length will get that fitting to turn.

Then we tried to put on the new hydraulic hose and found that we couldn't because both ends turned the opposite direction. Again I called Bill, who suggested getting a union fitting to put on one end. This would allow the joint to swivel. Yep, that worked just fine. Then, later, I looked at another of the hydraulic hoses and found a union on that one. Someone else must have had the same problem in the past. Now I'm smarter than I was.

The trailer is delivered

So we spent a week measuring the trailer site, leveling it, and shoving back the old logs even further into the trees, trying for a relatively flat spot on the gentle east-facing slope. After a couple of holdups, Bill called and told us that the trailer would come up the next day and that he had borrowed his friend, Andy's, larger tractor to help haul in the trailer in the event that Dale Sandberg, the driver and a family acquaintance, couldn't get it down our mile-long trail.

We had gone down the trail and cut out any leaning trees or ones that were too close to the road, hoping that our judgment was good. We didn't want our trailer ripped up or stuck part way home. A 14-foot wide trailer would take up every bit of our trail. It had rained, but the trail seemed pretty solid. Would the rig get stuck somewhere? And if it did, would we be able to get it out?

Later that day, David on his four-wheeler and me leading the way, Dale and Bill started down the trail with the, seemingly, huge trailer. It filled the entire trail, crashing over small trees and brush on both sides as it went. We all held our breath as it came on...and on. In about 10 minutes, the trailer was backed into its resting place in our yard. Bill was right. Shoved way back in the trees, you didn't notice it too much. And look at all that room. After living for six months in a 28-foot travel trailer and attached fish house, a 70-foot trailer looked simply huge.

Bill, Bob, and David blocked up the tongue and wheels very well to prevent our temporary home from rolling down the slope and we were in business. As the trailer had been used only for a hunting shack and weekender, the care it had received was not the best. The inside was basically solid, but there were rotten spots in the hall and bedroom floors, squirrel holes in the ceiling, mouse you-know-whats everywhere, and plenty of cleaning to do. Besides that, the insulation under the

Bob, Bill, and Dale Sandberg set the new trailer into its site.

trailer was pretty much gone and the roof had leaked. Yep, a fixer-upper. But that's what we do best, it seems.

We had bought several rolls of fiberglass insulation and had them sitting next to the site. So while Mom and Dad sat in lawn chairs, Bill, Bob, and David crawled under the trailer and began the horrible job of tearing out the old insulation and stapling new insulation between the floor joists. I acted as the gofer, opening bags of insulation and handing the appropriate sized batts. In this trailer, there were three sizes of openings between the floor joists, 15 inches, 22 inches, and 25 inches. This made things more difficult. A 16-inch batt would work for the 15-inch openings, and a 24-inch batt could be compressed to fit in the 22-inch opening, but we had to tape part of a 15-inch batt to another to make the 25-inch openings. This slowed things down considerably.

It took several weeks to get it mostly insulated, but the next week Bill came with a large air powered hydraulic jack and he jacked the trailer up just enough to get the wheels off that he had borrowed from his wife's uncle. About that time, a friend rolled in to remove the axles we said he could have if he took them off. We have no plans on ever moving that trailer again so getting the axles off made it easier to insulate and block the trailer up on its cement block piers. When our new house is done and we move in, we will use the mobile home as a guest house and storage for our "too much stuff."

Like a hive of bees, we clustered around the trailer, Bill jacking and leveling, David, Bob, and I carrying cement blocks, handing a shovel to Bill under the trailer to level the spot each pier sat on, finding blocks of two-inch planks to finish out piers to be perfectly level, and other gofer jobs. We worked very carefully, as that trailer weighs several tons and we had no desire to end up squashed under our home like the witch in The Wizard of Oz.

Flooring and doors

As soon as we had the trailer squared in as low as it could possibly sit, Bill packed up his equipment and got ready to head home. About that time, Mom and Dad wanted to see the inside of their new temporary home. So we lifted Mom's wheelchair up through the front door and Dad climbed gingerly up the cement blocks we'd piled as temporary steps in front. Aided by three of us, they were in. Inspecting the unit, front to back, both were full of ideas for remodeling. Like I said, the five of us in our little travel trailer was cozy. This seemed to be a battleship.

But so much work to do. First off was to shore up the rotten spots in the floor. That turned out to be easier than we thought. Most rotten spots were at the edges of the trailer due to water leaks. We just had to sandwich one or more two-inch planks along the floor joists to support a new piece of plywood under the flooring. This we screwed snugly, using a battery powered power screw driver.

This is one of the handiest tools we own on the homestead. We have two, one a 9-volt and the other a 12-volt. Bill uses an 18-volt unit, which has much more power and lasts longer between recharges. We use ours for some job nearly every day of the week. The big bonus over using nails is that you can later remove something, without damaging the building material. It seems that we're in a constant state of changing from temporary to permanent, building to rebuilding, and the screws save time and material.

In front of the front door was a large rotten spot, due to the door being fit incorrectly. The previous owner had added an exterior storm door, which had no flashing. The water poured off the roof, down in between the doors, and ran into the house. Pretty soon, the flooring had rotted. To fix that, we used a stud finder to locate the floor joists on each side of the rotten spot. Then carefully adjusting our circular saw to cut just a tiny bit deeper than the flooring was thick, we marked out a four foot square to remove the bad flooring.

The lines were drawn down the center of each floor joist, then across them at right angles. Carefully holding the saw down firmly in front, with the rear elevated and the guard held very gingerly open, I started sawing, slowly lowering the saw to meet the line and moving forward as I did so. This neatly cut through the flooring to the wall. Then I turned around and finished the cut past where I had started. Repeating this on two other cuts, we were ready to remove the flooring. David got under the trailer and with a hammer and pry bar, he loosened the chunk until we were able to pry it loose above. Being rotten, it broke up in several pieces, but it came off, leaving nice straight edges.

While I measured and cut a new piece (which we'd scrounged at the dump), Bob and David nailed in short pieces of header (2x6) to support where we'd cut across the floor joists, as the flooring had to be supported all the way around.

It only took a few minutes to nail the new flooring into place. Now you don't fall through the floor when you come into the door!

Speaking of the door, the Mickey Mouse storm door fell off in my hand the first day we had the trailer home. It's lucky it didn't fall off on the highway. Our friend, Tom, who got the trailer axles, saw the bad state of our front door. The frame had pretty much rotted away due to the same water leak that had done in the floor. Tom's a pretty handy guy, doing carpentry, roofing, and all manner of other fixer-upper jobs for a living.

A day later, here came Tom with a complete door and frame he'd taken out on a job. Grabbing a saw, tape measure, and hammer, he, Bob, and David set about tearing out the old door and installing the new one. Whew, could that man work! In an hour, they'd completely installed the door and he hung the curtain that came with it. And the door actually closed all the way.

He did more or less what we did with the floor. He cut out all the rotted wood, carefully saving the inside paneling and outside aluminum, cut studs to replace the vertical studs that had supported the door frame, tacked the sheeting back onto it, and slid in the door frame.

Once we could keep heat inside the trailer and critters out, we set about getting it ready to live in it as soon as possible. Mom and Dad's bedroom floor had been sheeted with plywood underlayment, as it wasn't rotten, but was weak in spots. They bought a roll of vinyl flooring to cover it so it was my job to get it ready to put down.

This was a little tricky to cut as there was a built-in set of drawers, a closet, and one wall was two inches off square when the trailer was built. Using a large square, I determined that the outside walls were nearly square. Then, using them as a starting point, I very carefully took measurements for everything. Two days later, I measured it again and checked my figures. All were correct but one, which I remeasured and changed. You know the old adage "measure twice, cut once?" It is so true.

We have no flat, smooth place to lay out linoleum, so we hauled it to a grassy meadow half a mile down our trail and unrolled it carefully. Then with a permanent marker, a straight, 10-foot long 1x3, and a yardstick, I marked the cuts, praying they were right. Again, checking everything over, I was satisfied they were correct. Sweating mightily, Bob and I cut the flooring, using a pair of straight tin snips and a linoleum knife.

Rolling it up again, we were off for home. Preparation of the floor consisted of covering a hole where a floor vent had been, filling cracks where pieces of plywood had joined and sanding them, vacuuming, and covering the areas with a few sheets of newspaper to prevent any possible wearing.

To do the job right, we should have used mastic, but this flooring may be taken up later to use in a bedroom in the house, so we just laid it without cement. Carefully starting with the roll in the square corner without a closet or other cutout, we unrolled and kept tugging the flooring perfectly straight. So far, so good. Then came the closet and its cutouts. Bob has more patience, so he crawled in there and puttered around with a linoleum knife for perfection. Not bad. Then we fit it around the drawers. Ouch, we were two inches shy. How could that have happened?

I was frantic until Bob pulled the side of the cabinet back out. It was poorly built and someone had pushed it in during the work. Whew!

We were done and it actually fit.

I cut carpet bars for the bathroom door and the hall doorway to keep our feet from ripping up the edges of the vinyl. Add some trim to the walls, and we're in business. Not perfect, but suited to our purpose. And the room looks a hundred times brighter and much cleaner.

Heating

Okay, now they had a bedroom. But the nights were getting cool and Mom freezes when it's 75°. We needed heat in the trailer before we could move in. And you can't use a mobile home furnace without electricity. Running the generator 24/7 is not an option.

Dad has bad lungs and cannot tolerate wood smoke or even aftershave lotion. So we couldn't use a woodstove, which isn't safe in a mobile home anyway. Our other option was to install a vented propane heater in their bedroom, and plan on adding another one before real cold weather hit in the living room. They are expensive, but with elderly parents, we had no choice.

Dad bought a smaller unit at our local Fleet Supply store and Bill, who is a certified gas technician, installed it. We could move in without having popsicle parents.

Being located on top of a hill, with the surrounding land relatively clear due to a clear-cut timber sale 10 years ago, we get quite a bit of wind. And we didn't want the mobile rocked off its piers in a strong gust. So to stabilize it further, we set about to start skirting the trailer. This prevents wind from getting under it and lifting. It also keeps it warmer in the winter. We just used pieces of plywood siding that we had scavenged at the dump and cleaned up. I screwed the top to the outside floor joist of the trailer and where the pieces joined I screwed them to vertical pieces of 2x4. As Bob and David insulated a section of the trailer I added the skirting on both sides. The front I beam sat right on the ground.

Building an access

Two days after getting the mobile set up on our site, we celebrated Dad's 93rd birthday (and my nephew, Sean's 15th birthday) in the bare-bones trailer. To get in, we carried Mom's wheelchair up through the door and helped Dad, with his cane, climb the rickety stack of cement blocks we were using for a temporary stairway. That was scary, but Dad is stubborn and wanted in.

So, to avoid future problems, we set about to add a deck and handicap ramp to our new, temporary home. Measuring eight feet out from the trailer, we dug two three-foot-deep holes with a post hole digger. (To get them square, we also measured 10 feet apart, then measured diagonally, like an X. When both measurements were exact, we had the marks for our holes.) Then we tamped in the two treated 4x4 posts that were eight feet long. Using a level on both sides of each post, I made sure that they were straight, all ways as they were set.

Then we screwed a 2x6 onto the outside floor joist of the trailer. To make sure this was the right height (so the deck would be exactly level with the mobile's floor), I held a scrap of decking on top of the 2x6. I screwed the end near the door first, with Bob and David holding the 2x6 and a level. Then we did the other end and center.

Holding a piece of decking on this plank, we held a level on it, establishing where another 2x6 would be screwed to the outside of the posts we had set. Then we leveled this one, which would support the outside edge of the 8-by-10-foot deck. We also ran other 2x6s from the posts to the 2x6 on the trailer to box in the bottom of the deck, then every two feet, from one end of the 10-foot deck, to the other. This would securely support the decking.

After this was done, we simply screwed down the decking. David loves helping on such projects. He got his start back in New Mexico. At five years of age, he helped Grandpa make two other decks, using a power screwdriver before he could ride a bicycle.

We had the deck complete in two hours, and then started the ramp. I screwed a piece of 2x6 down across the top of what would be the head of the ramp, holding it down ¾ of an inch, so the ramp would end up flush with the deck. Then we screwed a 16-foot 2x6 against the trailer on a gentle slope, with the bottom resting on a piece of patio block flush with the ground. The bottom of this plank was beveled, to sit flush with the ground. We did this kind of trial and error, but finally got it right, cutting two to match.

Mom in her new home

The second formed up the outside of the ramp. We dug in three more posts, which would support the cross pieces under the ramp and would also hold the handrails. We found scraps of 2x6 here and there, cutting them to fit every two feet across the ramp, and especially from post to inside (trailer side) of the frame.

Then all that was left to do was to screw down the ¾-inch treated plywood, making a solid, gentle access ramp for wheelchairs, canes, and walkers.

This ramp was completed in less than a day, including the handrails. But I will admit that at the end of the afternoon, we were all pooped. Bob opted for a nap and I asked David if he wanted to go with me in the canoe out on the big beaver pond.

He seldom turns down canoeing, and minutes later we were paddling across the still water. We had not been on the big beaver pond since

David and I check out the big beaver pond after work.

spring as there were many water-fowl nests that we did not wish to disturb. We were especially interested in what had become of the Canada goose nest on a hummock near the beaver lodge. The last time we'd been on the pond, there had been six eggs clustered in a batch of goose down. Had they hatched or had a predator gotten the eggs?

Quietly we paddled to the nest and found the remains of six hatched eggs. The babies were hatched. And by now we knew they were not babies any longer. Geese grow quickly.

We sat on the pond for quite some time, as the sun went down over the pines. Beaver swam curiously around us, trying to find out what that strange creature was on their pond. They came very close and looked us in the eyes. Then whack! Their tails would smack the water in the alarm signal. But in a few minutes they were back, scarcely able to contain their curiosity.

It was nearly dark when we began paddling slowly for home and there in the flooded, dead trees, we saw the family of geese, all in a line moving slowly on the golden water. Mom, Pop, and all six babies. Only the babies were colored the same as the adults, and very nearly as big. Months pass quickly here in the backwoods. ✍

Chapter Four

$\mathcal{L}$ate autumn was upon us here on our new homestead in the remote northern Minnesota backwoods. And we were busily readying for the long, cold, typical Minnesota winter. After all, winter is one reason that there is still much wilderness up here. (If it weren't for the lengthy, snowy, bitter winter and the bugs in the summer, all of our 10,000 lakes would be built up, elbow to elbow, and the woods nearly so.)

With a bare-bones homestead, there was much to do and money was tight. We worked long into the evening one day, hearing of a snow storm headed our way. All day we had picked up stray tools, fencing, building material, buckets, and anything else that the snow might bury. Often, when the first heavy snow comes, it does not melt away, but is with you until breakup in April. A tipped-over shovel or anything left unprotected simply disappears until spring.

Then there were the animals to weatherize. The partially built goat barn was nearly done, but we threw two sheets of plywood on that part of the roof that was unfinished and screwed them down for protection. Then David ran to the house for two green plastic tarps and the staple gun. By cutting one of them in half, we stretched plastic over each gable end to keep out the snow and wind and hung another down over the door. Animals can stand very cold temperatures if there are no icy drafts blowing down on them. The metal roofing would have to go on, as far as it would go, if this snow did not stay long or the storm did not come.

Working by flashlight, we stuffed straw into the unfinished openings between the rafters. And as we walked back to the house, the first snowflakes began to blow through the cold night air.

We live our lives according to the weather radio, listening to it the first thing in the morning and the last thing at night. This was a habit we had developed when we lived seven miles off a road, a thousand feet higher than the continental divide, back in the Elkhorn Mountains of Montana. Being snowed in from the first of December to mid-May, our travel plans hinged heavily on the weather. The only way down the mountain during the winter was via snowmobile. And with David only a little guy, I stayed home when Bob went down to gather our mail, gas, and supplies. I can't tell you how many mornings he had planned to snowmobile down to "civilization" on a bright, sunny day when the weather radio strongly advised otherwise.

Storms can come up in less time than it takes to think about them and one needs to be prepared for what they will bring. In Montana, we simply hunkered down, brought in more wood, tightened up the livestock, and I baked bread and cookies while Bob read. And, likewise, here in Minnesota, we live our lives around the same little $12 weather radio. We feel it is foolish to disregard what Mother Nature is about to hurl at you.

So we continue to listen, watch the skies, and prepare. Even the wildlife prepares for storms. We have noticed that when the deer get up midday and forage hard or when our bird feeders are suddenly swarming with more customers than usual, we can expect a change for the worse in the weather. Sort of like when you look up and see a huge ring around the moon—a sure sign of changing weather with moisture.

The next morning, I opened one eye at a time, expecting solid white outside. What a surprise to learn that the storm had swung south of us at the last minute. But it was a good wake-up call for us, knowing that winter was pretty darned close upon us.

Putting in the well

So we continued to prepare. Mom and Dad wanted to contribute to our homestead, as they were now members of our backwoods family.

Dad bought an old Jeep pickup truck with a rough but useable snow-plow on the front and had me call a well driller. While we worked on the Jeep, getting it ready to plow the drive this winter, I hoped KO Well Drilling from Cook would get their big well rig out before the snow was too deep. We plan on hand-drilling a well off the hill down by our garden. But after talking to several knowledgeable people, we bit the bullet and called a well driller for our house well. It seems that there is a lot of granite ledge rock in the area and many wells, especially those on high ground like our home site, run right through hundreds of feet of solid rock.

Well drillers charge by the foot. In our area the going rate is $22 per foot with another $15 a foot for steel casing. Whew! But Mom and Dad were adamant. We were going to have a well.

We hadn't heard much from the company, but one bright, cold morning they called and said their truck was on the way out. I'll admit I was a little (no, make that a lot) scared. In Montana, we had a well driller come out and he went down 385 feet and hit only a trickle of water, basically a dry hole that took hours to fill part full with water. And we had sunk over $5,000 into that hole.

The huge red drilling truck backed into our well site that we had chosen for ease of drilling and because it was about halfway between our temporary mobile home and our new homesite. This site would enable us to run water to both homes, as well as to the goat barn, where we will put a frost-free hydrant.

They set up and began to drill. Each length of drill was 20 feet, and I stood and watched while the pile of drill pipe stacked on the side of their truck shrunk all too quickly. By noon, they had run down through 87 feet of gravel. But right after lunch, they ran into the dreaded ledge rock. (Dreaded by me, at any rate.) Shades of the hole we had drilled in Montana.

Well, the guys drilled and drilled, having to quit at four o'clock, down 260 feet and still nothing. The day was clear, but bitter cold. They would be back the next day.

And so they were. Well, they drilled and drilled, ending up at 325 feet. Luckily, there had been cracks in the ledge rock, and trickles of water slowly filled the well. It wasn't a super strong well, but it would more than meet our needs.

A week or so later, we had a submersible pump dropped down the well, and we were in business, netting five gallons a minute for many hours' pumping. We felt fortunate to have good water, too, as much of the well water in our area is orange with iron and minerals. (We are north of the Minnesota Iron Range, where much iron is mined.) To prevent our well pipe from freezing during the bitter cold, we drilled two eighth-inch weep holes in the plastic pipe, down 10 feet. These drain the water out of the pipe, down to below frost level, after the pump is shut off. So it is a freeze-proof well.

We had lucked out. It was still relatively snow-free. But deer hunting season was upon us. And we still had to put the sheet metal on the goat barn roof.

David's first deer

David was excited. Although he had been taught from an early age to shoot both a bow and arrow and rifle, by both Bob and me, he had to take rifle safety classes to get his first hunting license. He did that during the previous summer and received his certificate. And because he runs the woods nearly every day, he knew where the deer came and went and what they did all day. He came home one day, just before opener with the news that he'd found some good buck rubs down by our creek, quite close to his deer stand. Buck rubs are a very good indicator of deer activity, not only of bucks, but also does in the area, for if there aren't does during rutting season, there certainly won't be bucks. Those rubs are cleanly skinned smaller trees and brush, usually down about knee level. Often the ground in the area is also stamped and trashed as he goes about his ritual "fighting" poses. "Take that! And that! And if that isn't enough, I'll really rough you up!"

All summer David and his cousin, Sean, had improved the huge, old deer stand, using it for a hangout, but now the stand was going to get serious.

The first two days of deer season, David spent the entire day out in the woods. He saw many deer, but the only buck he saw provided him with only a fleeting glance, and he'd been taught for years not to shoot when there was no clear shot and not to shoot a running animal. There are too many deer to hunt to risk a poor, wounding shot.

David finds a good fresh buck rub: white scar, sap still wet, and shreds of bark.

David went out before daylight, using a flashlight to find his way. At first he hunted the woods over on state land and Potlatch timber land, keeping away from his stand. Then he decided to go to his stand about an hour before sunset. Being the anxious mom, I worked about the house, listening. Wondering. He was using my old Winchester Model 94 .30.30. It's a good gun for the woods, light and easy to carry, and dead accurate.

I was washing the dishes, watching the shadows lengthen. Wham! I heard my rifle bark. Just once. We'd taught David to wait 10 minutes after shooting a deer before going after it. (A deer that will lie down and die after being shot, might, on pure adrenaline, still run at the sight of a human. Running just a few hundred yards can make it impossible to find.) So I bundled up in my blaze orange, grabbed a flashlight, and kept an ear out for another shot. Nothing.

I also waited 10 minutes, then started walking down towards the deep woods where his stand is located. On the way down, I whistled once and he yelled back. The whistle doesn't scare game, and if he'd needed to he would have whistled back. He had either clean missed or had a deer laid out.

One look at his smiling face as he walked to meet me told the whole story. The 14-year-old had his first deer. And it was a very fat, nice fork-horn buck, too. This is our favorite age and sex to hunt. The meat is wonderfully tender and flavorful. He is also easily spared in the breeding needs of the local herd.

And I was proud of David. He'd fired one shot at about 150 yards, neatly dropping the buck with a heart shot, right in the trail. There was a lot of meat lying there ready to haul home.

By flashlight, we dressed the buck, propping his front end up on the snow so gravity would help us. Using Bob's nifty skinning knife with its razor sharp four-inch blade, I held the skin up and carefully inserted the tip into the lower abdomen, next to the scrotum. Once into the abdomen, I kept the sharp edge of the knife towards myself, guiding the blade with my fingers inside, slitting the belly from scrotum to brisket. Then with my sharp hatchet, I chopped the pelvis bone carefully between his hind legs, while David held his hind feet apart to ease the operation.

David and his first deer.
A proud moment for us all.

54

Once that was cut through, I carefully reached up into the body cavity and opened the diaphragm and reached as high up into his lower neck as I could. Very carefully, I severed the windpipe. Then I handed David my knife and began pulling the insides down and out. With gravity working for us, it did not take much touch-up work here and there with the knife before the gut pile slid out onto the snow covered ground.

We wiped out the cavity with piles of snow and loaded the buck on the sled, heading for home. There, we also rinsed out the body cavity very well with cold water, propped the cavity apart with a willow stick, and hung him on the side of our stock trailer. It is very important to clean out the body cavity, both of blood and debris, and to cool the carcass quickly. (In our yard, there are no trees large enough to hang a deer and the bears were not yet hibernating, so the stock trailer was used.)

The next day I skinned the deer and began canning the meat. I cut one hind quarter off the carcass with a sharp knife and a few strategic whacks with my little hand ax. Luckily, the meat was partially frozen, just perfect for cutting. When it is warmer, the meat does not cut nearly as well, being "sloppy" to handle.

David wanted me to make the whole deer into jerky, but I talked him into letting me can up a bunch of stew meat, as well. Yes, he does love jerky. I sliced the meat into boneless steaks, carefully trimming away any membrane, fat, and gristle. I'll admit I'm a fanatic about meat; it must be clean and nice. Every jarful.

Then, as I use stew meat in so many recipes, I diced the steaks into pieces about three quarters of an inch square. I used to put up my meat raw, to save time precooking it. But I've found out that it tastes and looks better when precooked. It is also more tender. So I got out my largest cast-iron frying pan and, using the least amount of vegetable oil possible, I stir-fried the meat until it was nicely browned. Then, adding water to cover it, I mixed in two tablespoonsful of powdered beef stock. I like this broth over venison. Even people who "hate" venison gobble down my "beef" stroganoff and other dishes.

*Trimming the steaks takes time,
but results in very fine canned meat.*

Once the meat is mixed well with its broth, I dip out the meat, filling the jars to within half an inch of the top. Then I dip up enough broth to fill the jars to the same level, covering the meat. Then, after wiping the jar rim clean, I place a hot, previously boiled lid on the jar and screw down the ring firmly tight. The jars are processed, at 10 pounds pressure for 90 minutes, in my huge pressure canner. I have to laugh, because I've canned at 10 pounds pressure, at altitudes below 2,000 feet, all the way up to 14 pounds pressure way up in our Montana mountains. Now, I have to think a minute before processing.

I used to can most of my meat in quart and pint jars. But now I've learned to can very little in quarts and much more in half pint or smaller jars, as I use less meat in mixed dishes, using the meat more as a flavoring rather than the main ingredient. It's healthier and the meat goes a lot farther. You scarcely notice there's less meat, either.

Then I sliced up a backstrap to use in David's favorite jerky recipe. Most recipes say to use "cheaper" cuts for jerky, but that results in tough, stringy jerky. We like the backstrap or tenderloin better and the jerky is very tender. I slice the meat across the grain, making it more tender, yet. While some of my jerky is in the "traditional" strips, more is in little discs from the tenderloin or small end of the backstrap sliced straight across. This makes jerky rounds or chips. They are very good eating.

I slice up the meat and place it into a glass bowl. Then I add about half a cup of brown sugar, one teaspoon of garlic powder, half a cup of soy sauce, one tablespoon of onion powder, half a teaspoon of coarse black pepper, a tiny bit of roasted chili paste, and a few drops of liquid smoke. Mix the meat well with this, cover and store in the fridge overnight, then lay the pieces on a dehydrator tray and dry at about 140° F until nearly dry. Turn and continue until they are stiff and leather-like. Or do as I do and hang them on a cake rack in your gas oven, using only the pilot light, and dry until done. You must place a cookie sheet under the jerky to catch the drips or you'll make a mess of your oven.

You can store the finished jerky in a canning jar, in the fridge, or in the freezer. Old-time jerky was dried much more than you'll enjoy— nearly like sticks of wood. When there is a bit of moisture left in, the way most folks like jerky today, the jerky will not last too long at room temperature and will begin to mold.

David had a quart of his new jerky gone in a week's time, but I figured he'd deserved it, bringing home the bacon, so to speak.

Roofing the barn

In between canning the deer, we hit a period of nice warm, sunny weather and got busy screwing down the sheets of green metal roofing we had stacked out next to the goat barn. As it is simply not safe walking on barn roofs that are icy and snow covered, we'd waited until the roof was clean and dry to get at it, feverishly hoping that would happen yet, before winter set in.

David got on the roof with a 12-volt power screwdriver snapped to his belt and Bob and I carefully handed up one eight-foot sheet of roofing at a time. (You don't want to do this with any wind blowing, as they want to take you sailing.) With an eighth-inch drill bit in another power driver, David quickly positioned the first piece and, while we held it from ladders below, he drilled several pilot holes to receive the roofing screws. In the past we'd tried to simply drill them in through the aluminum roofing, but it took forever before the screw would bite and pass through the metal. And you can't pound a pilot hole with a nail or punch, as it will dent the thin roofing.

The screws are driven in the top of the ribs and are screwed in tightly enough to flatten the rubber washer that comes with them somewhat, but not so much that the roofing is dimpled. This would allow water to pool around the screw and possibly leak.

We were able to put up three sheets the first day before our power drivers were out of batteries. It sure would be nice to have extra batteries for such things. The next day, we hauled our generator out to the site and simply used a regular drill, fitted with a Phillips bit to finish the job. It was quicker and no worries about running out of battery. Just weather. It was starting to snow in earnest.

The east side of the goat barn is still sheeted but not covered with metal roofing, but as soon as the spring thaw begins that, too, will be finished.

David learns to plow

Our first major snowfall dumped over a foot on us, and we still have it on the ground, buried under several more feet. David had been practicing driving the old Jeep plow truck here and there in the yard, moving it as needed. At first, of course, he couldn't get the hang of the clutch. But because he had used Bill's tractor during the summer, it was only a few minutes before he was cruising around smoothly. I envy these country kids, learning to drive around their own land before hitting the highways. When I learned, it was driver's ed in high school and crowded roads from the first. I was terrified.

David was dying to plow our mile-long trail, and when that foot of snow fell he just about dragged Bob out into the truck for a trail run. David and the old Jeep did a great job. The trail was clear and as nice as blacktop. The smoothest our trail becomes is during the winter when the ice and snow fill all the little ruts and pockets.

The one thing he soon learned, however, is that one must plow extremely wide at first because during the winter, with more and more plowing, the trail becomes narrower and narrower. Pretty soon there's not much of a place to put the snow; it simply falls back onto the road. The first few times I plow, I begin plowing outward from the center of the road, then work further and further toward the woods, as you would if you were sweeping the snow off with a broom. This makes the plow banks nearly at tree line, not just off the roadway. Plowing this way leaves quite a bit of room to stack snow on subsequent snowfalls.

Another lesson I learned years back is not to create plow banks on the upwind side of the drive in areas that are clear and wind blown snow is a problem. Banks catch blowing snow, acting like a snow fence, dumping huge snow drifts across the road. It is much better to plow only to the downwind side. Then if drifts form, they are heaviest way off the road.

"I'll plow it out a lot wider, next winter," he said. He had learned. Another lesson he learned was not to race the engine when plowing on ice.

He took the truck out of the yard with the rpms up way too high one night, trying to plow deep snow, with an inch of ice underneath. I yelled and yelled, but of course he couldn't hear with the engine revved up so high. But the truck seemed to even out and down the trail he went.

But he didn't come back.

We took the Suburban out to find him, cringing to see the Jeep in the trail with the hood up and a puddle of oil under the engine. "It started making a clanging noise…" David peered into the engine compartment. "And there's this crack or something…."

Sigh. He'd blown the engine. One thing I'll say for Bob; he never raised his voice a bit. "I guess you've learned not to race an old engine, huh?" David only hung his head and nodded. Lessons are sometimes hard here in the backwoods. ✤

Bob Clay 1946-2005

We are very much brokenhearted to tell you that my husband of sixteen years and best friend, as well as David's father and best bud, died suddenly of a brain hemorrhage. The night before, Bob and David had gone to David's karate practice, the Cook High School basketball game, and come home feeling happy and well. I woke up at 2 am with Bob having a seizure. He was taken by ambulance to the Cook Hospital, then airlifted to Duluth via helicopter.

Surgery was done to try to relieve the pressure in his brain, but it did no good. By 2 am on the 16th of February, only 24 hours from the onset, Bob died.

He was a *Purple Heart* Vietnam veteran who suffered from the effects of Agent Orange and post-traumatic stress disorder. But to us, and those who knew him, he was a quiet, special man with a wonderful sense of humor and caring ways. We may never know how many lives he touched, but after his death we received so many cards and notes, often from people I did not know, telling how Bob had always had time to talk to them and what a great guy he was. I was surprised, as we have only

Bob always had time for David. They were best buds.

been in the area for a year and didn't know that so many people even knew who we were.

During our life together, Bob always went ahead of me, breaking trail. I kidded him about it because he was part Cherokee and said the warrior always went first to scout the dangers to protect the woman. (He knew I could handle trouble as well as he could.) But he still went on ahead, stomping a trail in the snow while I padded on behind watching for tracks and nature signs.

It recently occurred to me that he is still going on ahead, breaking a new trail for me to follow someday.

It was Bob's wish that he be cremated and his ashes spread on a special place down by our creek

Bob was always going ahead of me and breaking trail for me, as he is in this photo when we went out and checked some wolf tracks. He still does.

where we feed the birds and other wildlife. David and I will be planting a small memorial garden down there for him when the weather warms.

And yes, we will remain on the homestead and continue with the dream Bob and I had from the start. With luck, we'll get that log home dried in this summer and plant a better garden. But it would have been better with Bob there to enjoy it. We will miss him terribly.

Chapter Five

$\mathcal{L}$ittle did I know when I began this series, telling of our family's building a brand new homestead in the wild woodlands of northern Minnesota, that the title "Starting over again" was to soon be doubly true for me. For on February 16th, I lost my husband, Bob, and would be starting my own life over again.

There is still family about me at home. I have my youngest son, David, as well as Mom, who is 89, and Dad, 93. But there is this huge emptiness in my life now. How many times I see something beautiful and turn to tell Bob, who has always been there. And there is just the wind.

This is my first experience with a close death. It is not an easy experience. One moment Bob and David are chatting happily, bantering about tonight's karate practice and only a few hours later I wake up with Bob next to me in bed, drenched in sweat, having a seizure, and vomiting. I feel his spirit left him then, for he never responded to anything thereafter. Not the ambulance crew, the doctors, or even David and me.

Massive brain hemorrhage. It sounds like something that couldn't possibly happen to a middle-aged man who is in relatively good health. No injury, no warning, just this.

And my husband and best friend laid in the hospital bed 24 hours later with a ventilator doing his breathing for him, and enough intravenous tubes running into his veins to make me wonder how they could possibly find room to stuff them all into his arms. The specialist had done surgery, removing a piece of skull to try to reduce the tremendous pressure in his brain from the bleeding, but he doggedly held absolutely no hope of any type of recovery.

I numbly stood and felt his words strike my heart. How could this be?

I held Bob's hand and talked to him for 24 hours, desperately watching the heart monitor, blood pressure, and oxygen readings. I prayed, I hoped, and waited. Sometimes his hand seemed to squeeze mine and I hoped even more. But deep down, I knew. I knew.

We had had the talks about not wanting to be kept alive by artificial means, ventilators and tubes, when there is no hope of recovery. But talk is easy. The decision was the most horrific one of my life. I fought it hard. I am not a quitter. But finally, the swelling in Bob's brain pressed so hard that it ruptured the brain stem. The doctor bluntly said he was now brain dead.

Even then, I held Bob's hand and hoped for a miracle. My oldest son, Bill, and his wife, Kelly, had come to be with us and had brought David down the two-hour drive to see his dad. Even earlier, I knew. But in those long dark hours of the night, I fought the decision and hoped. He no longer squeezed my hand and I knew Bob was not coming home.

I made the decision, feeling like a traitor. A murderer. And began to cry for the first time since it had all begun. They sent for a chaplain so I would not be alone when he died, and I cried as they removed the tubes and ventilator. We prayed, I held his hand, and cried like I've never cried before. He went from me quickly and peacefully, but it did not help.

I relive the day every night still.

Surprisingly, most folks' response, other than shock and sadness, of course, is questioning me as to what we will do now. I suppose they expect me to fold up the homestead, pack up my 14-year-old son and elderly parents, and move to town. Why, I just can't guess. Perhaps it's the old gender prejudice that says a woman just "can't make it out in the woods" without a man.

But I already know that's so much a lie that it's obscene. Self-reliance is not just for men, you know. We women can be quite efficient at it too! In fact, continuing onward with our new homestead is the one thing that keeps me going after such a tragedy. Of course, it's easier and a whole lot more satisfying to have your husband share it with you, but the truth is the way of life is just that. It's a path, a way. And all you have to do is put one foot in front of the other every day and you find yourself on the way. Even if you are alone again doing it.

But, thank God, I am not "alone," even though sometimes I feel lonely, hollow to the heart. I have my youngest son, David, with me, my folks at home, and other family within a couple of hours' driving time away. And I do have a great family and wonderful friends and neighbors, even though we're just newcomers to this area.

So what's to become of us? Simply, we are going on. Oldest son, Bill, came up with an old dozer he'd bought and cleared a good road out to our house site. By the grace of God, Bob had just been awarded 100% disability from the Veteran's Administration for his Agent Orange-induced health problems, which was retroactive to when his claim had begun years ago. Just two weeks before he died, we received a lump sum check, which Bob wanted to use to buy a 1960s Volkswagen and have a small log house roughed in by a local company. As we were

Mom enjoying her birthday (89th) with young tomatoes and peppers. Life goes on.

caring for my folks (Mom in a wheelchair and Dad on a walker), we just couldn't go into the woods for cutting logs to build the way we had planned.

It seemed as if it was meant to be. So we have our house in process. We'll still have to do a lion's share of the work, as Bob's check did little more than buy the basement and logs, stacked. But it will give us a good start.

Bill dozing off an old slash pile for another garden

The dozer also cleared my garden spot and opened up another spot of rich dirt next to the old mobile home we're living in temporarily. So I'm clearing gardens, picking rocks and old logs, sorting seeds, and planting flats of vegetables.

I guess it helps that I was divorced in prior life, having kids at home to raise. You soon develop a forward going spirit and learn ways of doing things, even though you are a "woman alone." Yes. That did help with this time of aloneness. But then, it's not really aloneness, at all. Having David to be there and help me is great. He was raised on wilderness homesteads for most of his life and was totally immersed in all aspects of it, right from birth. This young man is not your typical 14-year-old. He has developed real skills, from building, gardening, hunting, tractor driving, to logging and more. Bob is not here, but David fills in when he is not in school.

My son, Bill, who also grew up "doing," is a great supporter and advisor. He provided many, many suggestions on our house plan in order to get the most living out of a small house and to make it work well for us. He and his wife, Kelly, have visited often, sometimes bringing equipment and supplies, which helps boost my sad times.

*Just another woman seeking
a self-reliant lifestyle*

And our neighbors and friends keep popping in with saws and hammers in hand asking what project they can help me with today. It is so nice of them I can scarcely thank them enough.

At 58, I've learned a lot. I've had to. So may I offer a little of what I've learned to other women traveling down the self-reliant living path without a man at their side?

Start small and make a list

First of all, I've learned not to try to do everything at once. Getting a big flock of poultry, many dairy goats, cattle, sheep, and horses, building housing for them (and you), fencing, working up a large garden, and canning all of it just won't work. Add the caregiving necessary for children (or elderly parents) and the time window narrows even more.

It is awfully tempting to instantly become self-reliant by overestimating our abilities. You look at that great piece of land, just lying there waiting, and you itch to do it. But it just doesn't happen all at once, even with the constant help of a man.

I've learned to start small. Then work as you can, each day, toward a final goal. If you're a listmaker, by all means make a list of your goals on a dry erase board tacked in a prominent place. Use an outline form with your basic goals, such as **Big Garden**, then the goals broken down into priority "bites" toward that goal, through the years ahead. For instance:

Big garden

Make six 12 by 4-foot raised beds:

• Place railroad ties on ground.

• Fill beds with rich compost and rotted manure.

• Plant the beds.

 Or:

Rent, borrow, or pay someone to till garden spot.

Clear and till a 25 by 50-foot garden spot:

• Pull grass roots.

• Pick rocks and rotted wood off garden.

• Plant easy-to-grow crops on the new land.

Next: Make eight more raised beds, 20- by 4-feet each.

Or:

• Buy good used rototiller. (Or new, if I can.)

• Till up another larger section for next year's garden.

• Fence garden spots to keep deer and other varmints out.

• Build portable panels for trellising peas, pole beans, and other climbers to make more use of existing garden.

• Build a small greenhouse so I can start my own vegetable and flower plants.

Once you have the list, you can cross off each task as you get it done. This gives a visual, which is of immense importance. Especially when you are having a down day.

These lists should include nearly everything you hope or need to accomplish. Do not erase the tasks as you accomplish them, but cross them out or check them off in **red**. It is a great morale booster!

Enlist folks to help you when appropriate. I say "when appropriate" because it is very necessary not to fall into the habit of using people. When someone offers help, honestly and enthusiastically, accept with true gratitude. If you need help, call out to friends, family, or neighbors. However, make that a "once in awhile" event, not frequently. You can

Our friends and neighbors have been great. Here, Tom Richardson helps us start our new 10x10 greenhouse to grow garden plants.

do so much more than you think you can if you just keep at it and learn new skills. I learned to sweat-solder copper pipes over the phone with my Dad after my pipes froze and broke in the basement. It took a few calls and a little experimenting, but I can now solder with the best of them.

Remember that there are books and magazine articles available to teach you those new skills, too. When you see there's something a bit scary and new coming up on your list, do your research before you start. It's not so scary, after all. I've stumbled my way through so many "new" ventures that I laugh to even try to count them. And everything came out pretty much fine anyway.

Even your young children will enjoy being included in new projects. David was pounding nails in our kitchen addition when he was two years old and simply loved it. There are many appropriate tasks you can share with children. It makes all of you feel a part of the homesteading family. If there are no children, you can still share your homesteading life with interested neighbors, friends, or family. Self-reliance is not living a hermit's life. Although I would be perfectly happy living in an isolated chunk of interior Alaska, it's also great to share with others.

When to hire or barter a job done

If there are big jobs that are simply too much for you due to time, physical constraints, or other constraints, pay someone to do it for you. There are always folks around who pick up spare cash by hauling gravel, doing odd job carpentry, bulldozer or backhoe work. It is dumb to spend two weeks shoveling a ditch by hand when your neighbor would be tickled to do it with his tractor for $25. Time is so valuable on the homestead. In that same week, I could build a greenhouse, fence a goat pasture, and can two turkeys. Of course, this is providing you have $25. I've been broke, too, not having a dollar, let alone $25. I would still use the equipment to dig the ditch, bartering for the operation. For instance, trading two days of my labor doing fence repair in his cow pasture, or trading vegetable plants for his garden (I built the greenhouse, remember), or taking his kids to music lessons for a week. Get creative and save your back and time.

In New Mexico, to give you an example, I bartered with our neighbor, Earl Beard, to help on his ranch branding, vaccinating, and castrating calves one spring, in exchange for him bringing his tractor and post hole auger over to dig half a mile's worth of fence post holes. I spent two days at the Beard ranch, working cattle, and had the holes dug that would have taken me all summer to do by hand. Time is valuable on the homestead.

Stay out of debt

Finances are a bear for most women attempting self-reliant living. In today's world, charging seems to be a way of life. Buy a new car for monthly payments, buy a house with nothing down, have credit cards galore. It is a trap, and a huge number of people fall right into it and can't escape. It is deadly.

To become self-reliant, you must escape debt as much as humanly possible. This takes a huge amount of self-control, plus a huge amount of anger at what these "helpful" people and companies are really doing to you. All you need to do is to figure up just how much you will actually pay for that new car or new home with "low down payments and low monthly payments" or what your credit cards are actually costing you and you'll see red. I guarantee it!

Every day, I fight to chop down any debt. I have no credit cards. Our land is paid for in full. There are no loans, nor will I get one. Helpful folks have encouraged me to mortgage our 80 acres in order to have our new log cabin finished this summer. But, no. I don't feel comfortable getting back into that same tub of debt that I escaped from long ago. Who knows what the future may bring? My own illness or injury? Economic crash in this country? A terrorist attack disrupting daily living? We'll get the house finished. Maybe not this year, but it will get finished and I won't owe for its building.

Another thing that has helped me is to make a list of more expensive items you need to make your homestead work more productive or easier on you, in a prioritized format. For instance:

- Snowplow truck
- Troy-Bilt rototiller
- Tractor with front end loader
- Lumber for small barn

Then, as you get a larger chunk of cash such as an income tax return, or a lump sum payment from insurance or a summer job, plunk it down on the item on top of the list. I worked as a firefighter for the Department of Natural Resources for a couple of years during the summer fire season and used this lump sum check for such purchases. If you don't use the cash it will just be frittered away, leaving you with nothing to show for it. Get your priorities in order or you'll end up with a few meals eaten out, a few new clothes (that you could have bought for next to nothing at thrift shops), while not much has changed on your homestead.

Sitting out in our yard right now are a 16-foot stock trailer, a riding lawn mower that doubles as a homestead tractor, a 4x4 ATV, a snowmobile for winter access in bad weather, a big pile of rough-sawn lumber, the 30' travel trailer we lived in on our new homestead, and a Troy-Bilt tiller. All of these were bought using large lump sum windfalls of cash. (No, they didn't all come at once. The stock trailer is twenty years old!) This method works for getting you ahead. Slowly, but surely.

Likewise, I try to make one or two large purchases every month or so, as my money allows. Again, I use a list of priorities. This includes bulk foods for my storage pantry, fencing, garden supplies, or whatever. To do this, I scrimp like heck on other things, but it slowly allows me to get ahead. Last year I bought half of the metal roofing for the goat barn, steel fence posts, and enough wire for two strands around the horse pasture. Last winter I bought two rolls of field fencing and several bundles of steel posts for our goat barn, 300 pounds of flour for the pantry, and a case of canning jar lids.

Some things I buy when they are on sale, of course. Other things I simply buy because I know I will eventually need them and can now afford them. Then there is the alternative shopping I do, which saves tons of cash. Every time I get our local shopper paper, I quickly read through it for great buys in homesteading supplies. You'd be surprised what I've found: fencing for little or nothing, lumber, you name it.

Dumpster diving

Every time I go to the local dump, I check out the demolition dumpsters. I've come away with truckloads of 4 by 8 sheets of plywood, wafer board, lumber, windows, and more. True, the wood was full of nails in many instances, but we pulled the nails and saved over half of them to use. If you don't have a dump that allows recycling of building material, run a small ad in your shopper: "Wanted, building materials, free or very cheap."

Likewise, I almost never buy clothes for myself or my son, even at Wal-Mart. I've shopped at the Goodwill half-off days, the Salvation Army, yard sales, and especially at our Hospital Auxiliary Thrift Store on Bag Days where you can get a grocery sack, stuffed plumb full, for $2. And this store has donations from large income vacationers, so labels read Levi's, L.L. Bean, etc. Most are hardly used or even brand new.

Every dollar I save on food (which we grow much of on the homestead), clothing, and living expenses, I can sock in on our homestead.

71

By making investments in the homestead, I can increase our standard of living as well as safety margin, should world events take a dive.

If you'll look back, you'll see that none of this requires a man. Nothing against a man, you understand. I loved my husband of 16 years. But self-reliant living does not require a man's presence.

Tools for heavy work

There are a lot of helpful tools a woman homesteader will find nearly indispensable. Not all are expensive, but all of them will make life much easier. A simple moving dolly works for many more jobs than carrying boxes into a moving truck. I've used one to stack bales of hay or sacks of feed so I could pull it to the goat barn. And I've also used a truck dolly to haul cement blocks, flagstone, railroad ties, garbage cans, etc. Yes, I do have a bad back (had a horse rear over backward into my lap when I was seventeen), but life doesn't stop because of body weaknesses.

A garden cart with large wheels works even better than a moving dolly. The large wheels roll easier over rough terrain. And to load heavy objects, you just tip the cart on its nose and roll your load onto the cart. I've even hauled my 17-foot canoe on the garden cart by strapping the bow onto the cart with nylon ratchet straps and simply lifting the stern a bit and steering it around, pushing it ahead of me. Piece of cake! This also works with larger timbers, logs, and railroad ties.

A power driver, which is a battery operated drill/screwdriver, is so handy on the homestead, especially when you're doing it alone. By using screws instead of nails, you can change things around even after you've fastened lumber together, without tearing up boards as you can when pulling nails. For instance, we've just built a 10 by 10-foot greenhouse onto the back of our temporary mobile home. It's too nice to just leave there when we move into our new log home, so it is built entirely with screws so it can easily be disassembled and moved to the house. There it will become a permanent fixture.

I'm not selling rototillers, but there are two of them I really would hate to do without. One is my big 8-hp Troy-Bilt Horse, which is a hard working, heavy duty rear-tined tiller. This is my second; I wore out the first with 15 years of very serious gardening, including a three-acre market garden. Being a rear-tined tiller, it takes away most of the jump and hard to handle pounding a front-tined tiller dishes out. Women, especially, will love this factor. I know I do. Yes, you can actually walk quietly next to the tiller, just like the picture in the advertisement shows. (Be advised, though, that is when your garden has been worked up well, with most of the stones, heavy sod chunks, and branches taken off.)

My other tiller is a little 20-pound Mantis. This little guy is not a wimp. It is like tilling with a very mad weasel. I use it for in between my plants, to till raised beds, and to till small beds around the buildings. I also use it to dig tree holes and short ditches. You just walk it into the place you want to dig and pull backward slightly. By repeating this, you dig deeper and deeper. Then I shovel the loose dirt out of the hole and dig some more. You can dig a big fruit tree hole in about 10 minutes. Or you can bury an electric conduit, water line, or make an irrigation canal in the same way.

A riding lawn mower may seem to be a foo-foo tool, but I've used one for years, not only to mow extensive lawn (from which I save my grass clippings for the animals and for compost), but also to use as a garden tractor. I've hauled rock on our bad driveway with one pulling a small trailer. And I've hauled hay, compost, manure, mulch brush, and more. I've also dragged the driveway, using a wood pallet, to smooth out ruts. I've spread grass seed on the pasture,

David is a big help digging rocks and cheering me up, too.

73

David helps me finish the greenhouse.

hauled water to animals and potatoes out to the field. Of course, I've also used one to haul garden harvest into the house and to back into the aisle of the goat barn to clean pens.

A good pair of loppers (long handled pruners) is a good tool to have around too. I not only use mine to prune shrubs and trees, but also to cut small saplings to use as bean poles, trellises, etc., and to snip off corn stalks after they have finished producing so I can feed them to the animals. They also whack off prickly thistles, briars, and vines on the edges of your garden and saplings that want to grow in your pastures.

When you're feeling blue

You get the picture. A willing spirit and a few good tools will do much. But what about the times you feel so down, like you're the only woman in the world homesteading alone. We all have those times, especially when things are going wrong. The truck broke down, the hail got the garden, your relative says you're nuts for living like you do.

Get out and get some support. For me, this is a talk with friends who live a similar lifestyle, reading a few good magazines such as *BHM* or *Countryside*. Make an effort to find other women who live relatively close to you so you can visit with them on your down days. They'll probably do the same, using you to boost their spirits when they droop. No homesteading women close by? Get pen pals, phone pals. But have friends who are also homesteading under similar circumstances! When you're alone, you don't want to hear about how so and so's wonderful husband just built her a fabulous goat barn or fenced in her garden while she was shopping. You're already having a bad day. You don't need to be kicked too.

Time is the hardest aspect for single women trying to develop a self-reliant lifestyle. In the real world, we must have some kind of income to survive, but when we work a full-time job, it's awfully hard to drive home and homestead too. But it can actually be therapy for most of us. I did it for years, and was usually very glad to come home and dig in the garden or visit with my livestock.

Just know that a woman seeking a self-reliant lifestyle is far from alone. There are thousands of us out there. But we aren't the "norm." We are more unique. We feel the call, the challenge. And we respond with dreams and the vigor to make them happen.

Sometime maybe some bighearted guy with homesteading dreams will again walk beside me, listening to me point out the spring's first new wild flowers, will hold up the other end of the board, and will cuddle with me at night. But for now, my dreams of self-reliant living are still there and I'm working like heck to make them happen. ✍

Chapter Six

One thing I've learned is never, NEVER to say "What else can happen?" when things go bad. As if losing my husband, Bob, in February was not enough, I was told that tiny pea-sized lump on my elbow was cancer. Cancer! Me. How could that be? We live pretty darned healthy; I never smoked, drank, or did drugs. I take care in the sun, eat home-raised food as much as I can, and exercise by walking miles a day, digging, sawing, pounding, and all that goes with a homestead. So in addition to spring's normal hustle and bustle, I began a grueling schedule of first a radical surgery on my elbow (a nine-inch incision for a pea-sized bump!), radiation, and chemotherapy. Luckily, the pea was my only spot, which brought great relief; the elbow is easier to treat than lungs, liver, and a lot of other places.

But with bad things, there are always the good. Throughout all of this, I was planting seeds, tilling the garden, and watching our new house take shape.

Starting seeds

In our little 10'x10' greenhouse, I was able to start a huge array of plants for our gardens. Not only did I start several varieties of early season tomatoes, including Early Cascade, Early Goliath, Oregon Spring, Sun Gold, Lemon Boy, and a new hanging basket tomato called Tumbler, but I also started broccoli, peppers, watermelon, muskmelon, cucumbers, and my wonderful Hopi Pale Grey squash that is now nearly extinct. Of course, I also started hundreds of different flowers to cheer up the place. Food feeds your body; flowers feed your soul.

By raising your own plants from seed carefully chosen for the attributes that matter most to you, a garden is much more successful than if you go to the garden center or discount store to buy your plants. A tomato is not the same as any other tomato. Some are very good tasting and extremely productive, and some (the ones often seen in stores) are just cheap to grow. Some require 100 days or more after transplanting to set a crop of tomatoes, while others only take 52 days. In a cold-season area, those 100-day tomatoes just won't make a crop.

Likewise, choosing seeds for your garden requires a bit of study. I need varieties that produce very heavily so I am able to can them, ones that taste great, and are early to produce.

I've learned that in cold-season gardening, you can raise watermelon, muskmelon, and squash if you start them indoors like you do tomatoes and peppers. I plant three seeds in a foam drinking cup and write the variety on the side. Then I place the cups, with a small hole punched in the bottom, in an old roasting pan. This keeps them from tipping over and allows excess water to drain from the cups to water the roots later

on. I've used peat pots, but the foam cups work much better. Perhaps it is extra insulation on the roots, keeping them nice and warm on cool nights.

By planting the peppers in early March and the tomatoes in mid-March, they are ready to go into Wallo' Waters in early May here, when normally you wouldn't plant them outside, unprotected, until mid-June. We nearly always get a **very** cold night right about June 15th.

I plant the tomatoes and peppers in deep plastic trays that a friend collected for me. Mine are actually discarded

In our little greenhouse we started hundreds of plants.

David fills Wallo' Waters around the tomatoes.

sterile containers that held instruments and materials for surgery. They're about four inches deep and grow wonderful roots. Smaller containers are easy to handle and will raise all the plants the normal gardener could wish to grow, letting you separate the different varieties with ease.

In my containers, I plant between eight and ten tomato or pepper seeds, spaced carefully so as not to waste seed. Nearly all of them germinate. By starting the seeds in trays, you do not have to transplant later on into a larger container.

I always place my containers of planted seeds, which I've watered with very warm water, in a plastic bag to conserve moisture. This is usually a bread bag but can also be any small plastic bag, twisted shut. These are then placed in a high, warm spot. I'm always careful to check the containers every day after planting because sometimes those seeds that aren't supposed to germinate for a week to ten days pop up in two or three. If you don't check and get them into the light as soon as they sprout, they will become leggy and delicate and never amount to much.

As we have no heat in the greenhouse, I was carrying plants out in the morning and back inside in the afternoon for several weeks. At first there were only tomatoes, peppers, and geraniums. But by the time it was safe to leave them out there all night, I was really glad to stop hauling dozens and dozens of flats of plants twice a day.

Our new home

About this time, construction on our new log house began. Our mile-long trail through the woods was still muddy from spring breakup, but we had worked hard on it last summer and even the biggest trucks were able to get in. We decided to use a good local log builder to do the basic shell. Bob and I had always done everything ourselves and I felt like I was wimping out by letting someone else do the grunt work, but it couldn't be helped. This was the only alternative that would let us have our small home, especially after Bob died and my bump exploded my life. I couldn't work with one arm in a sling and stitches up and down my arm.

So the only choice was to have a not-quite-dried-in shell. When you buy from a log builder, there are many ways to go. You can just buy the logs, have them delivered, and stack 'em on your own foundation and sub floor. I couldn't even do that. (Well, I probably could have, but Mom and Dad would not have been able to enjoy living in it, as it would have taken years.) You can also have the foundation contracted out, along with the sub floor, then have the logs stacked by the log builder. By the grace of God, we had just enough money from Bob's retroactive VA disability payment to have the logs, including the ridge pole and rafters, stacked on the sub floor and the roof boards nailed on. On top of those, we stapled Typar roof wrap, a woven

The logs came numbered for ease of construction.

waterproof material that will last longer than tar paper.

Of course, many people have the house dried in by the log builder. This means the roof is finished with insulation and shingles or metal roofing, and windows and doors are also installed. But we can handle this, with help from friends and family.

Be careful when shopping for a log home kit. You need to find out exactly what is included. Some kits only include the logs for the walls. Others include the walls, rafters, loft floor, roof, insulation, windows, doors, and trim. You can't just pick the cheapest kit, thinking that all are the same; they're definitely not. Ask lots of questions.

With the brute work done for us, there will be plenty for me and David to do. And I wouldn't have it any other way or the house would never seem truly ours. This summer, David has grown up. At fourteen, he's a young man, not a kid any more. Not because it's been forced on him by the death of his dad, or by me making him do work I can't do. He's just pitched in where there is a need. And in doing so, he's won the respect of every man who's worked on the new house.

David first helped the masons lay up the block for the basement, mix and wheel cement, learning new skills every day. Then he worked in the rain all morning Saturday with the carpenter to lay the plywood sub-

floor. (Luckily, our friends Paul and Marcia showed up just after it began raining. I think the carpenter would have quit because of the rain, but together, they got the job done.)

The basement goes up.

We were really under the gun, since the logs were going to be delivered first thing Monday morning, and they were going to be stacked onto the sub floor. Luckily, Voyageur Log Homes has a crew that stacks logs and they have a big crane. This enabled them to lift pallet loads of logs directly off the trailers onto strategic locations on the sub floor. Not only did this keep the logs extremely clean but it let them stack the logs right where they would be working, saving much time and labor.

When you buy logs and plan on laying them up yourself, you usually are responsible for unloading the logs off the truck or trailer yourself. This entails either renting an all-terrain fork lift, a small crane, or using a tractor with a loader. You also need to know that the driver of the log truck will wait a specified time, then you will be paying him "overtime" for waiting for you to unload. Have help and work quickly.

It's best to stack logs on your slab or sub floor, but if that can't be done, at least have a deep bed of fresh straw to stack them on and plenty of tarps to cover them later, as logs weather quickly and get dirty even faster.

The logs usually come numbered or lettered if you buy a kit that is pre-cut. Stack all like logs together to find them easily when you put up the walls. You don't want to move piles of very heavy logs, searching for "log 12S."

The same day our logs were delivered, construction began on the walls. Scarcely were the logs unloaded when the half log ends were screwed over a foam sill seal with long log screws and the first full logs laid snugly over them. Voyageur Log Homes uses a notched corner and a full two tongue and grooves on each log. Caulking tape is fastened to the tops of both tongues, all the way down the log's surface, then the next log is settled tightly down onto it, with its grooves sliding snugly over the tongues. There is no chance of air leakage.

We've always done log work with a Swedish cope, where the top log is grooved broadly to fit down over the top of the one below. But Voyageur's system is extremely air tight and quick to go up.

David quickly began helping Mark Carlson, the log builder, and his helper. Three men build much faster than two. David is a good workman. He began taping the caulking down on the logs, and was soon hooking logs with tongs for the crane to lift in place, carrying shorter logs, and helping set them into place.

The first day, the walls were half up, and by evening of the second day, they were done. I was amazed. Even our log chicken coop had taken Bob and me all spring to build.

But I did notice many similarities in construction. We, too, used a heavy maul to "help" the logs fit into place tightly. Where we used long spikes, counter sunk two inches to allow for settling of the logs, Mark used Oly log screws, also countersunk to allow for settling. No log building is ever built that has no settling, and I've seen many that were nearly ruined when builders did not allow for it.

For instance, over every door and window you must leave a space so that when the building settles it does not bind, jam, or hang up on them. Stairs to a loft or upstairs must be slotted to let them slide an inch or two as the home settles through the months. Kitchen cabinets need to be fastened firmly to one log, with a slot or other allowance made for the logs to compress without being held by the cabinets. (I've seen ugly log damage from bowing and twisting caused by a single piece of 1" x 4" trim in the wrong place to allow settling.)

Last of all that day, the large, full-length log was hoisted into place as a collar tie, spanning the width of the house. This will prevent the long log walls from bowing outward years from now. It also greatly strengthens the entire home from snow loads and fierce winds.

When it came time to set the log rafters, on day three, Mark quickly manufactured a jig out of a few scraps of lumber. This jig was screwed to the flat top of each rafter, and his chainsaw slid neatly along the angled piece of 12"x12". This gave him an exact angled cut for each and every rafter with no monkeying around or climbing on the ridge pole to precariously cut rafters way up in the air.

The rafters were then lag screwed together and raised up onto the walls with the crane. Pretty slick! And pretty soon all the rafters were in place and the ridge pole was easily raised up under them with the crane. One by one, the pairs of rafters were straightened and lag bolted securely to the ridge pole. And soon, all that remained was to add a pair of large support posts under it.

Under the lower end of the post is a steel plate foot with a heavy steel threaded rod and nut. The rod fits into a hole on the bottom of the post and the nut with its heavy washer can be turned down as the house slowly settles. This keeps the collar tie beam and ridge pole nice and level.

We were sad when it came time for Mark to leave. He had become family and was truly a joy to work with, cheerful, and happy to share log building tips.

The next day, while I went in for minor surgery to have my chemotherapy "port" installed below my collar bone, the carpenters arrived to nail down the 2" x 6" tongue-and-groove roof boards. As the lead carpenter was "all business," David didn't get to help much, but he acted as a gofer and still managed to learn a lot.

By the time I got home, the roof was done and they were stapling down the roof wrap. Amazing. None of this was cheap, and knowing that hurt

The higher the walls went, the harder the work to get them layed up.

The rafters go into place. Note the lag bolts in the top, ready to screw into the ridge pole later that day.

my severely Scotch blood, but I was glad to see our house standing there, looking like a house.

We had planned to make a small partial base-ment under one end for a water handling area and place to store my canned goods and garden harvest. The rest of the house would be on cement piers to save money. But it turned out that for $1,800 more I could have a full basement. I gave the nod, and I have never been sorry. It added so much useable room to the little house that it's unbelievable.

There will be a small wood storage room for the woodstove in the basement, the water handling area with a place for the wringer washer, ample space for my canned goods and root cellar, a place to store all those boxes in storage right now, and even a small corner that David has claimed for "his" game room. I certainly can't deny him that.

I am so grateful for what we have, but I still feel that I didn't sweat enough to deserve it. I only wish Bob could be here to enjoy it with us.

Bigger, better gardens

While the construction was going on, I worked on the gardens. My son, Bill, more than doubled the size of our "lower" garden with his bulldozer.

Before I had surgery, I tilled the house garden next to the mobile home, then David gave it another tilling before I began to plant. One end was very rocky and he used a crowbar to dig out rocks as he worked. I was pretty much useless after my surgery, but after it was tilled, I slowly brought out a few plants and planted them or a package of seeds and gritted my teeth while I dragged furrows to plant them. Definitely this was the slowest I've ever planted a garden in my life.

The good thing is that it makes me appreciate everything so much more. The tiny steps forward, the sunsets, the wildflowers, the fragrance of spring turning to summer in the northwoods, the birdsong in the growing pines around us, my family. Everything. We all take life too much for granted.

Because our house garden is not large, I've planted things in square-foot style for the most part. For instance, I planted my sweet corn in a sixteen foot by four foot bed, with seeds every six inches, all ways. Then, to hopefully deter the ground squirrels who dug up my corn seeds when the plants were six inches tall, I surrounded the bed with discarded window screens from the dump. So far the corn is up, and the little buggers are staying away.

Likewise, I've set in a four foot by six foot patch of broccoli, with the plants a little over a foot apart; squash, watermelons, and muskmelons in another bed. To further save space, I used an extra sixteen-foot stock panel fastened to steel T posts from the dump as a trellis for cucumbers and pole beans. I planted a dozen foam cups of cucumber plants, complete with climbing tendrils started, along one end of the trellis and a double row of Cherokee Trail of Tears pole beans (our favorite) on the other end, on both sides of the fence. These are beans that Cherokee women sewed into their skirt hems and carried in their pockets during the awful forced march from their homes in the south to Oklahoma "Indian Territory." There are few beans that taste as good.

When you don't have a lot of space, it's a good idea to garden up, so I am trellising anything that I can. Watermelons and muskmelons don't climb, but can be gently tied and encouraged to sort of climb on pieces of fence wire stapled to pole garden panels.

Because this new garden, which last spring was a pile of rotted logs, is oddly shaped, I have tucked other vegetables in at different spots; green peppers in a four foot by four foot bed, yellow Romano beans in another, a row of Provider bush beans along the tomato patch, a little tiny row of radishes here and a few odd seeds of this and that all over. That little garden is jam packed with edibles. And it is on the highest piece of ground we have. It is safe from all but the most dangerous cold, as cold is like water, flowing down to lower ground first.

Like I said, everything in the garden took so long this year because of all the running around we must do and the lack of normal energy and strength on my part. But we got both gardens in, albeit a bit later than usual.

The new "big" lower garden is now planted with three hundred-foot rows of potatoes, two of Yukon Gold, and another of Norkota russet, which keeps very well. The Yukon Gold we simply laid on the tilled bare ground and covered with old straw from around the trailer this winter. The plants will grow nicely, free of weeds, and when harvest time comes all you have to do is fork off the straw and pick up the clean potatoes. I even sneak around the plants and harvest a few new potatoes after the vines bloom to have with creamed fresh peas and bacon crumbles. This is always an awesome meal.

David and I also planted three hundred white and yellow onion sets, two long rows of carrots, and two rows of Provider bush green beans.

We really need

The roof goes on, four days from sub-floor to house.

to get this garden fenced. The deer won't bother it until fall, but then they will harvest it for us unless we do.

Because of all the rain and unseasonable heat here this spring and early summer, everything is growing like mad, including all our bountiful wild fruit. I've seldom seen blueberries and wild raspberries so large and plentiful. This year I'll be canning plenty of fruit and jam, plus doing a whole lot of berry dehydrating. I can't wait! ❦

Chapter Seven

Summer has been a little crazy here on our new homestead, but rewarding nevertheless. The first wild geese are arriving from the north and the white-tailed deer fawns are losing their spots. It seems like spring was just yesterday, but I guess that's how it gets when you are busy.

With me undergoing radiation and chemotherapy in Hibbing, nearly 30 miles away, (all for a pea-sized bump on my elbow), it seemed like I was getting nothing done. My mind was tearing away with things to get done and my body was saying, "Go away, I want to lie down!" I couldn't believe I was taking two long naps every day.

But with my son, David, pitching in on a lot of my chores and other work, friends (especially Tom, the carpenter who I hired to help on the house one afternoon a week), and my son, Bill, coming up weekends, things have progressed.

Bill has been established on his homestead for over five years now, and having built a big, gorgeous log home, he's been there, done that, and has accumulated a lot of necessary tools and equipment, not to mention experience.

Early this summer, not only did Bill show up one Sunday morning, but he also brought his father-in-law, Donny. And behind Bill's truck was a flatbed trailer hauling Donny's little John Deere dozer. Our new log home was in severe need of backfilling so we could safely get in and out, without walking a plank over an 8-foot deep, 10-foot wide "moat," and Donny had volunteered to bring his crawler and help Bill fill the moat and grade the yard.

With time out for lunch and very few breaks, they changed our new, rough yard into something we can work with. The 12-foot high mountains of gravel turned into a gently sloping front yard. With Bill on his Ford tractor and Donny on his crawler, they pushed dirt, graded, and designed. I could only sit on our four-wheeler, with my chin on the handle bars, watching and answering questions as they came up. Finally, Donny's back gave out (he'd had surgery last winter), and Bill jumped on the crawler and David took over the tractor, using the back blade to help grade the yard.

Donny is an artist with his crawler and likes things nice, so after a break for his back he mounted up again. By late afternoon they had graded an entrance for a walk-in basement, a level front and side yard, and the moat was only a memory. Now it was easy to get into the house to work on the inside. Thanks guys.

Bill takes Donny's crawler down through the front yard.

Work begins inside

Because I was so tired from my treatments, I couldn't handle a hammer or a saw, so my job was trying to keep things flowing. Tom came every Saturday afternoon to do his carpentry magic, so I tried to keep ahead of him, rounding up materials he would need, making sure the generator was full of gas and at the house before he came, and making plans for what I needed him to do most.

Because he is more experienced at building than I am, many of my plans were tentative and changed as the day progressed. One of these was the use of some 3x10-inch beams Tom found at a local sawmill to use as floor joists for the upstairs. Logs would have cost three times as much and these huge beams were rough sawn, strong, and fit in with our logs just right.

After framing the walls downstairs with rough cut lumber, Tom began fitting the beams into the logs. All the time we were building, we had to keep in mind the settling of the log walls. Every time you build with logs, no matter how dry they are, they will settle.

We were told to expect from two to three inches of settling in our log walls, so Tom couldn't simply spike the partition walls to the logs. Two options were to cut a notch into the log walls to receive a 2x4, which will let the logs slip down it as they settle, or to cut slots in the upright 2x6 that framed the partition wall so the spikes could slip downward as the logs settled, yet keep the wall in

Tom begins laying the floor.

place. We chose this second option.

Likewise, Tom knew the log walls would settle, so initially the beams were set two inches high on the outside walls, which would keep the floor level as the house settled.

To set the beams into the wall, he and David snapped a chalk line from one corner of the house to the other, marking where the bottom of the notches to receive the beams would be. Then Tom marked out the sides and top of the hole and cut the sides with a carefully held circular saw. Using a three-inch hole bore, he drilled out a set of three or four holes. In a few minutes, working with hammer and chisel, he had a perfect notch.

They were so tight in most cases that he and David had to use a maul and block of wood (to protect the end of the beam) to drive the beam into the log.

The other end of the beam rested on a stoutly constructed 2x6-inch bearing wall, with the beams coming directly over upright studs.

One Saturday they got half of the house done, and the next, they nearly finished. It was slower the second Saturday because they had to frame around the stairwell to the upstairs.

The next Saturday afternoon, Tom finished our beams and he and David constructed the stairs going up to the bedrooms. The treads were made of the old planks we had used to walk across our "moat." They were cracked, but Tom suggested temporary treads until the construction phase was past because the stairway is the first thing you see when you enter the house, and he didn't want them all dinged and scratched.

As it turned out, this was a good idea because all the tools and materials going up and down those stairs did result in dropped boards and many dents in the treads. When we finish, we'll replace the treads with nicer lumber.

During that week, Tom ordered the lumber for our upstairs floor. I chose to go with 2x6-inch tongue and groove spruce, planed on both sides. It was relatively expensive, but it would allow us to use the underneath as a ceiling in the downstairs rooms and the finished floor for the upstairs bedrooms for David and me. There would be no additional costs for drywall ceilings downstairs or flooring and underlayment for the upstairs. This ended up to be cheaper by far than doing it the "traditional" way, using rough-cut 1-inch lumber or plywood. Neither of these is cheap today. An added bonus is that because the 2x6s are tongue and groove, it stiffens up a floor quite a bit. It looks great, too.

It was an exciting day when we came home to find that the lumber truck had been here and the delivery men had stacked the piles of lumber neatly upstairs where they were going to be used. This was a huge labor saver for us and there was no extra charge.

When Saturday rolled around, Tom showed up with his huge red work truck full of tools and began hauling out saws, power miters, and air nailer. Slowly at first (it is hard working with no room at the eaves), but faster and faster, the flooring was laid. The lumber was in 14-foot and 16-foot lengths. Tom varied the cuts to save every inch of material he could, and staggered the butt joints so that no adjoining runs of flooring had butts on the same floor joist. This makes a stronger and much more attractive job.

I had always nailed tongue and groove lumber by hand and was amazed at how fast a job Tom's air nailer did. I learned a neat trick, too. Inevitably, you get a bowed piece of flooring. I had always nailed a block onto the floor joist and used a pry bar to force it into place so it could be nailed. Tom has a better way. He cut a five inch or so scrap of 2x6-inch flooring on a diagonal. One piece he nailed with several nails to the floor joist, a few inches from the last board, then he set the loose wedge into the space and drove it in with his hammer, firmly securing the floor board into place. Then, with two hands free, he could take his time and nail the flooring into place. It only took him a few seconds to drive the temporary wedge out and remove the nailed mate. Of course, he saved this and reused it, time after time.

The first day he laid two thirds of the flooring. It took more cutting and fitting around the stairwell. I can't tell you how nice it looks, and what a boost it gave to our sense of "home." David and I sat out there the next day, enjoying the view from the gable end that was still open and unsheeted, planning how the bedrooms would go.

The next weekend when Tom showed up, I mentioned I couldn't wait to install two windows I picked up for the gable ends. (This end faces west, where our wind and rain usually come from.) Currently the window openings were covered over with the Green Guard wrap that also protected the wafer board on the gable end.

In less than half an hour, he and David had the windows carried up, unwrapped, and installed.

And on they went with the flooring. David was the generator man. When Tom needed power for the saw, it was "David! Power!" and David would dash down and crank over the generator. Tom would measure and saw a pile of flooring and then tell David to "Kill it!" This saved gas, and made it much nicer to work in quiet.

With the floor finally done and the windows in one end, we could see the light at the end of the tunnel. With a lot of hard work, we just might be able to get moved into our new house by this winter.

Tom and David continued working Saturday afternoons and got the east gable end framed and sheeted. I was able to pick up three Marvin windows at the local lumber yard for half price. I can only afford to buy a window or two a month, but slowly, slowly, the windows are stacking up and going in.

My son, Bill, said that when Tom finished the partition walls upstairs and the east gable end, he would come up and run the wiring. (He learned this skill by reading and re-reading a book on wiring, then wired his entire log home. Yes, it passed inspection.) So for three Saturdays, Tom and David worked at framing in the upstairs knee walls, closets, partition walls, and door openings. Time and again, Tom or I had neat ideas and we changed our initial plans, gaining storage,

*A rare Hopi Pale Grey squash
growing in our house garden*

ease of flow, and useable floor space. It's a small house, but we'll live big. (I keep looking for ideas in log home magazines and am horrified at the size of most of them. Who needs a 7,000 square foot log home to visit for a few weeks a year? I sure don't want to clean four bathrooms.)

My dad's 94th birthday fell on August 16 and my nephew, Sean's, was the day before, so we planned a big birthday party in the new house. Bill and Kelly came up on the Sunday before, bearing bags of junction and receptacle boxes, coils of wiring, and tools, not to mention a small gas grill, food, and birthday presents. The week before, Bill had instructed David to pre-drill holes in the upright studs to thread the wiring through, so the wiring would go quickly.

We took Mom and Dad in wheelchairs out to the house, and Bill and David carried them up the temporary steps and gave them the tour, even upstairs in the bedrooms. Then he set up his handy little grill and grilled the best hot dogs I've ever eaten.

My sister, Sue, and her son, Sean, were coming up the next day. Unbeknownst to Dad, my youngest sister, Deb, was driving up from southern Michigan for the party. It's been several months since my parents have seen Deb, so we knew Dad would be thrilled.

After lunch, Bill and David set about running wiring. It went so fast that by the time Kelly and Bill had to go, the wiring was all finished.

We were then ready to begin sheetrocking. My not-so-favorite task. Luckily, I had finished with my radiation treatments, and finally I was able to do something.

The next day Bill caught a ride north with my sisters and nephew and again we partied, complete with cake and more presents for Dad. My youngest sister thought we were completely nuts for building a log house; she insisted we'd be better off with a modular home. It'd be easier, quicker and less work. Yes, but I hate them and would rather build something that made me feel good about it. (Remember, if your family and friends think you're crazy for trying to live your lifestyle, you're not alone.)

The garden lives

While we were building and I was going through constant treatments, the gardens got little care. In fact, some of my tomatoes were not staked until they were four feet tall—some of them never did get staked. The watering was first done by heaven, as it rained nearly every day in the spring and early summer. Then the rain stopped and we went into drought for the rest of the summer.

We have a submersible pump in our well that puts out only about 3 gallons a minute, so it won't run a sprinkler, even way downhill from the well. To water the gardens, we pump water into our big 350-gallon poly storage tank next to the well. Then we hook up our gas water pump to pump the water onto the gardens. To get one inch of water on the gardens, it takes half a tank on each one.

Because we were so busy, the lower garden didn't seem to get watered when it should; I didn't even go down there because I was so tired. Finally, I decided we'd better water it and see if we could save anything. I had visions of dead, dried potato vines, deer-eaten onions and green beans, and brown tomato plants. So we hooked up the pump and walked down the hill.

I stopped in shock, literally. The garden looked terrific and it had only been watered twice that summer, with temperatures soaring to 100 degrees. The entire garden was green and growing. I had blooming potato vines taller than knee high, nice onions, green beans knee high and wide, and tomatoes loaded with green tomatoes and blossoms. It seems the angels had been watering for me.

So we soaked the garden with 350 gallons of water and went home with a thankful heart.

The gardens have continued to grow, despite the weeds, infrequent waterings, and nibbling wildlife.

Back to canning

A neighbor gave us two "out-of-date" spiral cut store hams she had bought as part of a case load deal, as well as several packs of frozen chicken. For the first time in a year, I hauled out the huge canner, hunted up clean, empty pint canning jars, and started canning meat. It felt good to be useful again.

I cut up the best of the ham and packed it loosely into the jars, leaving an inch of headroom. The rest I either diced up or packed in large chunks to use to flavor such things as baked beans, casseroles, or soups. Then I poured boiling water over the meat to within an inch of the top of the jars. After wiping the rim clean, I put on hot, previously boiled lids and screwed down the rings firmly tight.

These jars I processed in the pressure canner for 90 minutes. Every single one sealed nicely, leaving me to do the chicken.

This was a bit fussier, as I first boiled the chicken to get it off the bone. When it was cool, I de-boned all the chicken thighs, drumsticks, and wings. The bones and skin I put back

David is happy with our first crop of green beans in the neglected big garden.

96

into the stew pot with the broth to reboil. I added more water and seasonings: salt, celery seed, sage, powdered onion, and black pepper. While I cut and packed the chicken in pint and half-pint jars, I simmered the bones, skin, and miscellaneous discarded chicken. When all the jars were packed to within an inch of the top, I poured the broth through a strainer and discarded the bone pile into a dog-proof container to go in the trash. I dipped the broth out and filled each jar to within an inch of the top, then carefully wiped each jar rim. Chicken broth contains fat, which sometimes prevents lids from sealing.

Then, like the ham, I put hot, previously boiled lids on the jars and screwed the lids down snugly. The leftover broth was poured in the jars plain and the jars sealed as above. I processed the jars for 75 minutes at 10 pounds pressure.

All in all, I ended up with 36 ham meals and 18 chicken meals. This includes jars that were pint or half pint. Sometimes you only need a little meat for flavoring, and other times you need more as a major ingredient in a meal.

Two weeks later David and I picked our first string beans to put up. I planted several types of beans and we picked yellow Romano, green Romano, and Provider, ending up with a huge basketful to can. In fact, there were about three times more than I thought we'd have.

I love doing green beans, as they are so easy to can, and they quickly fill the jars with one vegetable that just about everyone in the world loves.

I sat on the sofa and cut off the stem ends and cut the beans into a big bowl. The work went fast, as the beans were so good—we'd only just picked them minutes ago.

When I was done, I set jar lids to boil, as well as a saucepan full of water to boil to pour on the beans in the jars. While this was going on, I filled the jars of beans to within an inch of the top, packing them down tightly. Raw packed fruits and vegetables float, leaving juice or water on the bottom of the jar; I could avoid this by hot packing them, but the raw pack is faster and I just wanted to get them put up.

By this time, the water was boiling in both pans; I turned off the jar lid pan's heat and began dipping water out of the pot to pour over the beans. (I added a teaspoonful of salt to each jar to enhance the flavor. It is not necessary.) Each jar was filled to within an inch of the top with water, then the rims wiped clean.

Sealing the jars was easier still. A hot lid was placed on each jar and I screwed down the rings fairly tightly. They were processed in the canner for 20 minutes at 10 pounds pressure. The time seemed to fly and they were done. Our first batch of Minnesota-grown green beans amounted to a dozen pints—a great start, and the garden is only getting better.

Right now, I have another batch of beans ready to put up, more than a bushel of tomatoes, red-ripe and luscious on the vines, and the potatoes…oh my! Just yesterday, David and I pulled back the straw from our Yukon Gold potatoes to peek, and looking back at us was a fist-sized yellow-gold potato all clean and shiny. And the vines have not even started to die down. We should have a terrific crop of 'taters to store in our new root cellar under the stairs of the new house.

After a spring and summer of pain and exhaustion, things are definitely looking up. But that's the way life is—continuous cycles of hard and easy, joy and sorrow. I can honestly say that I'm glad we're finally on the upswing now. I'm ready to walk the wooded paths and delight in nature again. &

Chapter Eight

Some days you wake up and start the day like a house afire. It seems like you never have the time or inclination to sit down and rest. That's the way our whole late summer and autumn have been. After finishing up with my radiation and chemotherapy treatments, I'm finally feeling like me again. As the summer progressed, I was able to do more and more.

I started off by helping David trim our goats' badly neglected feet. Dairy goats originated in rocky, desert, and mountainous country where they were herded from one grazing area to another. They ran, jumped, and climbed rocks and rough terrain, effectively wearing down their shell-like hooves. But when we put them into small corrals and pens and bed them with straw and hay, those feet grow longer and longer. Sometimes they break off by themselves, but most of the time, they continue to grow and twist. In some cases, they can permanently cripple a goat by forcing joints to absorb pressure in unnatural directions.

Goats should have their feet trimmed at least every six months. Ours had gone more like ten months and were walking on ski-like feet.

David had never done this job before, so one bright morning we took our goat trimming shears (sharp, pointy, pruning shears) out to the goat barn. All of our goats have been regularly trimmed and really don't mind. Even our big Boer buck, Rocky, and David's huge black wether, Oreo, have learned to jump up onto the milking stand to eat their feed while their pedicure is in progress.

We've learned it's easiest to trim feet on a nice day following a good

Supporting the goat's flexed leg makes trimming the feet easier on the goat.

rain. Walking around in the mud makes the goat's feet pliable and easy to trim.

To trim a foot, hold the leg up in a flexed position. With the trimmers pointed toward the toe, trim the excess shell off even with the bottom of the foot. If they are quite overgrown, as some of ours were, it helps to snip across the end of the toe first, then work back toward the heel.

Sometimes the heel of the foot has also grown quite long, so gently snip across that, if needed, a little at a time. This rubbery "callous" gives goats the surefootedness they are famed for, but it can get out of hand if left untrimmed.

You want the trimmed foot to look like the foot of a six-month-old kid. Nice, square, and neat. If you don't get it perfect the first time, go back in a week and take a little more off in strategic areas. We were lucky, and all our five adult goats' feet were quickly done.

That's not to say we're all caught up in the goat barn. Half of it is devoted to our small flock of Shetland sheep. These are an ancient breed of small sheep from the Shetland Islands. They are famous for their hardiness and the softness and high quality of their wool.

Unfortunately, we still have not given them their Spring shearing. That is on the list for next week. Luckily, they have a nice warm indoor stall to stay in until their wool grows back.

The house progresses

For a long while, every time I wanted to grab a hammer and start finishing work on the house, I had no energy. So the only major steps happened when our carpenter friend, Tom Richardson, came on Saturday afternoons.

Windows in a log home are tricky to install. Like everything else, consideration must be given to the settling of the logs. Although they were air dried, our logs were expected to settle about 3" overall. So we couldn't cut a square in the logs and nail a window into it.

With a chainsaw, Tom cut the initial window openings to size, snug on the sides and 3" larger on top to allow for settling. Then he cut a vertical slot in each side, to receive a 2"x 2", trimmed the same height as the window, again leaving room at the top for settling. This was not nailed in, but bedded in fiberglass insulation, so that the logs can slide down this spline as they slowly settle.

This slot was outlined and rough cut with the chainsaw, then further opened up with a chisel and hammer.

Once the vertical splines were both in place, the window was shoved into place and nailed to the splines. The space above the window was stuffed with fiberglass and will be covered by temporary one-inch trim until the house settles.

The sides of the windows were also stuffed with fiberglass, because caulking can retard settling. When the house has settled, they will be caulked as well.

Because setting windows and doors this way is so tiring and

Our Shetland ram waits for shearing day—6 months late.

I'm mudding screw heads.
My hair is growing back finally. Hooray!

labor intensive, Tom would do a window or two, then hang sheetrock for the remaining hours he worked each Saturday afternoon.

I knew I was feeling better when I began to hang some smaller runs of sheetrock during the week. I also bleached the roughsawn 3"x 10" beams on the ceiling of the first floor. They'd been stacked outside for months, and many of them had weathered to a dark gray. It was a dirty, blotchy look that definitely had to go.

Back in Montana, I had cleaned up some log siding that was mildewed and weathered badly using chlorine bleach. It had made the wood look like new. So in a hidden area, I sprayed bleach on my beams with a spray bottle. In minutes, the timber lightened right before my eyes. Another hit with the bleach and it was almost like new. I spent a couple of weeks spraying bleach on overhead beams. Some took three coats, but they all turned nice and bright.

Then I began taping and mudding the walls. I was about a day into that when a new friend of mine showed up one morning with her husband. Jeri and Jim wore old clothes and were all set to sling mud with me. Any job is more fun when you have company. We visited, taped, and spread sheetrock compound on my new walls.

We had all hung sheetrock before, but it had been a long time, and with a little helpful criticism from Tom, we learned a lot. I already knew that the sheetrock screws must be indented, but not so far that they tear through the paper. We were using too much plaster over the screws. Tom showed me how to use a larger knife and rub a little compound across the screws, then go back and level it again from a different direction, leaving very little compound on the area. This results in much less sanding in the end.

You can't just lump sheetrock compound on a screw, then sand it down. You have to give each and every screw three separate coats, allowing each one to dry thoroughly. This was easy for me; I made one pass over every screw on a wall or two, and I was ready to rest for a while.

Then there was taping. Like the screws, we started off using way too much plaster to bed and cover the tape. This made a lumpy joint that was tough to sand. Instead, I found out that if I used a wide knife and smeared the compound across the joint, then leveled off the excess by running parallel to the joint, this left just enough to let the tape bed well. Then I cut off enough tape to span the joint, stuck one end down, and carefully ran the knife over the tape to squeeze it over the joint tightly. When this was done, I again smeared compound over the taped joint for a few feet, then went back and leveled it off, running parallel to the joint and bedding the tape into a thin layer of plaster.

Another thing I learned was to try to use factory edges next to each other at any cost. This resulted in much smoother joints, as the factory edges have a little indentation along them, allowing you to bed your tape neatly in plaster that fills it evenly.

I no sooner got the sheetrock done upstairs that I got the itch to begin painting. My son, Bill, and his wife, Kelly, gave us the leftover paint from their newly built log home, and luckily our taste in colors is similar. Almost all of the walls in their house are finished in earth tones of beige, cream, and buckskin, with wallpaper borders of moose and deer.

The stain for the logs and the spruce ceiling was a different ball game. I knew what color I wanted, but just couldn't find it anywhere. I think I looked in every paint store in northern Minnesota, only to end up finding it at our local hardware store in Cook (population 600).

I wanted our home to look like it had been around awhile, not just built. So I wanted the golden brown color of mellow, old pine. And I found it in a tung-oil based stain that showed the glorious grain and knots in the wood to its best advantage.

Let me tell you, it was a bear of a job to brush all those gallons of stain on the rough sawn beams and ceiling, but I've learned that you get stuff done by keeping at it, no matter how huge the job seems. The first day I got half a wall done, being careful to thin out the brush strokes and end each log in a different area so that I didn't double up on the stain and create a darkened, obvious overlapping. I also got one side of one beam and one section of ceiling stained in the living room.

I was trying to use a sponge brush, as I was instructed, and it was a miserable job. The next day, I had no more sponge brushes, as the rough wood had torn all three to pieces, and only had a cheap three-inch paint brush. Because I didn't want to drive to town, I used the brush and was pleasantly surprised at how much faster the job went. I got three sides of beams done that day, two lengths of ceiling all across the living room, a whole wall, and the leftover half wall from the day before.

A week later, the entire bathroom was stained, and all but one little strip in the kitchen. It looks fantastic. I'm so glad I finally found the right stain instead of settling for something else in desperation.

The potato patch yields

As the nights were growing colder and colder, with the aspen leaves a bright yellow, I knew it would only be a matter of time until we had to dig our potato crop. If you wait too long, any potatoes that lie close to the surface will freeze or chill badly, resulting in rotten potatoes.

So one sunny afternoon after a frosty morning, David and I went down to the potato patch with a garden fork and buckets to dig our crop. We had planted two rows of Yukon Gold potatoes under straw, and two rows of russets in the soil next to them. Unfortunately, due to our hugely busy summer schedule and my lack of energy, the russets had never been hilled. Hilling your potatoes increases the amount of potatoes in each hill as potatoes are generated from the lower stems as well as the roots; the more stems under the soil, the more potatoes you harvest. This also seems to work with the straw-covered potatoes. I usually heap more straw on the plants as they grow, and the straw compacts onto the soil. But I never got around to doing that this summer, and I wondered if we'd actually make a decent crop.

David caulks all the cracks he can find before gable ends are insulated and finished with log siding.

Boy, was I surprised when we turned over the first straw-covered hill and five bright gold potatoes the size of my fist rolled out onto the ground. Not all hills were so productive, but most were and we quickly filled a huge bread bowl and five-gallon plastic bucket. David jumped onto his ATV and went home for more buckets.

Again, when we started on the row of russets, I wondered if there would be any potatoes of edible size because they never got hilled and were only watered three times all dry summer. While David was gone, I stuck the fork into the hill on the far end of the row and out popped six huge potatoes. Bakers for sure and not a little potato in the hill.

Down the row we went, excited as little kids. We love to dig potatoes, and we were very happy with the four buckets and huge bowl of perfect spuds from such a neglected garden.

Putting the garden to bed

A garden is hope in earthly form. In the fall, you already are planning on next summer's crop and must get ready for it. This is a good thing for me, a cancer survivor. As soon as the potatoes were dug, David cleaned up the compost pile with our little Ford tractor.

This huge pile, which included manure from the goat barn, had composted down to half its size, but was still a considerable amount of compost to add to our new hillside garden. The soil there consists of about eight inches of rich, old woods dirt on top of gravel. It will be a great garden with a little help. The gravel and gentle hillside ensure good drainage, and the woods loam and compost we will add through the years will make it fertile and productive.

Working carefully, David scooped up the compost with the tractor bucket and spread it out to cover most of the garden's surface eight inches deep. This is about how much manure our Troy-Bilt

David harvests potatoes from our neglected garden.

tiller will plow under at one time.

This spring, we bought eight-foot-long steel T posts just before the price went up. If the weather holds out long enough, we'll get those in the ground before it freezes to keep the deer out of the garden next year.

This year, they ate all the carrot tops, resulting in stunted carrots, and ate and pulled the onion tops. We quickly harvested all our onions from on top of the ground, where the deer had conveniently left them.

Luckily, the deer left alone the beans, sweet corn, potatoes, and best of all, our precious, rarest of rare, Hopi Pale Grey squash. Although small, our few vines produced six mature squash. This squash is so rare that only a handful of people raise them, and only one Canadian seed source is currently available.

Just last week I cut one in half. There were fat, mature seeds in the hollow center, and a lot of them. I sat down and carefully picked them out of the strings and laid them on a cookie sheet to air dry. By the time I finished with that one smallish squash, I had the sheet full.

We hope to be in our new house by the time winter sets in, and are working daily to make that happen. Although we will eventually be powering our home by solar panels on the roof and heating it largely with wood, at this time we must continue to heat with propane. The time and money ran out before we could get the foam insulation, sheathing, and shingles on the roof, as well as the chimney built.

The Typar roof wrap was not keeping rain out of the house when it blew hard and I knew that winter would only be worse. Not being able to afford a finished roof, I picked up two huge heavy duty construction tarps (the silver ones, not the lighter-weight blue variety) for $200, and Tom stretched them out over the roof one afternoon while we were in town. I was so surprised when we got home. It looked like an alien space ship had landed out on our point. All that silver, where a black roof had been that morning.

The next time it rained, the inside of the house was bone dry. What a relief. The roof had been leaking so badly that it was actually raining

All windows and doors are installed, a ramp for Mom and Dad is up, and we are dried in. Two 30' x 50' tarps on the roof finally keep the rain out.

about as bad in the living room as outdoors.

Now that we have a plastic roof, using any type of temporary wood-stove is not an option. Any flyaway sparks could land on the poly tarps and burn our house down!

Having a mile-long logging road for a driveway, it's sometimes hard for the propane truck to make a delivery mid-winter, so the gas company suggested that we put in a thousand gallon tank to see us through without a fill. I agreed, but now propane has gone up over $2 a gallon. We'll just have to fill it as we can afford it, and hope for a relatively snow-free winter. It seems that we do everything as little as we can, and pray we have time to do more before it is needed. We call it homesteading here in the backwoods and we thrive on it, knowing that we owe no one for what we are creating. No one but our neighbors, friends, and family who share their work, talents, love, and encouragement with us. Without that we would have a hard time going on. ₰

Chapter Nine

Winter is what keeps Minnesota underpopulated. With more than 10,000 lakes, gorgeous forested hills of pine, maple, aspen and fir, the state would be elbow-to-elbow built up if it wasn't for its reputation for snow and cold, sometimes reaching less than 55 degrees below zero. But to tell you the truth, we actually like winter here. The snow-covered trees are gorgeous, and we feed the birds so we always hear birdsong and find new feathered folk at our feeder. The fresh snow tells a story in animal tracks each and every day that you wouldn't know about in the summer. The strike of an owl on a roosting grouse, the passing of a pair of wolves, otters playing go-slide-down-the-icy-creek, a moose crossing the trail: It's all there for us to "read."

I often go to Bob's memorial garden by the creek, in the woods down below the house. As a Vietnam veteran suffering from PTSD, he spent his life searching for peace. Stationed in Okinawa after two tours in Vietnam, he became interested in martial arts and Oriental philosophy. So after he died, we searched for a statue of the Buddha to place on a rock surrounded by flowers where we scattered his ashes. Bill found a statue in Australia (Bob'd love that!), had it shipped, and it now sits on a huge boulder in the woods. I feed the birds down there and enjoy the serenity of the Buddha in the snow. (Neither Bob nor I is a Buddhist.) While winter is long and sometimes hard, there is always a certain peace that is soul-refreshing.

And winter keeps us indoors more often, allowing me to get more done to finish up our new log home. Yes, we did get moved in! This happened in December, just before Christmas. The first of the week I checked the propane tank of the mobile home we were "camping" in. It had been cold, and it was getting down there. So, I called the gas company. By Wednesday they hadn't shown up, and I called again. Excuses. A truck had broken down. By Friday we were *really* getting low and so was the temperature. I called first thing that morning and was told we would get delivery "for sure." I dialed down the thermostat and waited. No truck.

Saturday morning we were down to 2%, and I knew we had to do something. The log home had 200 gallons of propane in the tank, but the basement heater could only keep the house at 60 degrees....not enough heat for my elderly parents. So when our carpenter friend, Tom, showed up to work on the house, we set about frantically moving. This entailed hooking up and moving our propane kitchen range and fridge as well as a wall heater for Mom and Dad's bedroom.

Then we had to move my parents' bed, clothing, and everything in the mobile home that would be harmed if it froze. We hurriedly boxed all of the home-canned goods in the large pantry, under the sink, and in the cupboards, plus all of Mom's store-bought canned goods—and on into the night.

The new house, midwinter

We drove Mom and Dad down to the house, then continued hauling boxes. By eleven o'clock Tom left and we were ready for bed. Thank you so much, Tom. David slept in a chair in the basement and I slept on a mattress in the bathroom. But we were moved in, and we were *warm*. Not to mention exhausted. I was beyond tired, but it felt so good to finally be home.

Hauling hay

We have goats, sheep, and three horses to feed. And because we have no barn storage, we find that feeding big round bales of hay is better than small square bales. Pound-for-pound, round bales are cheaper to buy. And because they are rolled up with a round top, they shed rain and snow moisture well. Only the "cap," or top and bottom, gets bleached and ugly. The rest is sweet and delicious to our stock. When you pile square bales up, it is very difficult to protect them adequately, even if you tarp them. You have the best luck piling them on wood pallets, then using heavy-duty tarps all the way around, fastened down with bungee cords. But sooner or later a cord breaks or comes loose and the wind rips a tarp, letting in moisture. And pretty soon, you have moldy hay.

While sheep and cattle can eat hay that has a little mold, even dusty hay is very bad for horses; they often end up with a respiratory condition that resembles emphysema in humans, called "heaves." This is very difficult to overcome and often the horse can never work hard again. Goats will frequently bloat from eating moldy hay.

So, because we have no dry hay storage area, we feed round bales. Now these bales weigh about 1,500 pounds, so you can't just roll 'em around to where you want them, or even dump them handily out of the back of a pickup truck. We get our hay from a friend who is also a local farmer. The easy part is getting the hay loaded onto our truck. He lifts it into place with the front forks of his big tractor.

At home, we must unload it. As we have handled these huge bundles of hay for years, we've developed techniques that make the off-loading nearly as easy as getting them on to the truck. We always carry two logging chains in our old blue Chevrolet pickup. One is 30' long and the other is 15'. One way we've unloaded rounds is to wrap the long chain around the bale, with the hooks on the cab end of the bale. (If you put the hooks on the tailgate side of the bale, when you dump the bale, the

After a whole lot of rushing,
we got moved into the new house.

hooks end up under the 1,500 lb. bale and sometimes it is very difficult to get the chain off!)

With the tailgate either removed or unhinged and dropped down all the way, you can use a short chain or even a heavy-duty ratchet strap hooked to a stationary object and the chain around the bale to gently pull the bale back to where it is getting almost ready to fall off.

Then simply back to where you want to unload the bale, back up quickly, then apply the brakes. The bale will dump out neatly. (If the bale is rocking or you have a distance to drive, you can use the heavy-duty ratchet strap from one side of the truck, over the cab end of the bale and ratcheted down to the other side to hold it in place safely.)

For a stationary object, we've used a tree, a boulder, and even our Suburban. Just hook securely and gently pull away slowly.

Round bales store well on their sides, with the "cap" up to shed rain. Once they are on their sides, rain and other moisture will quickly enter the bale and rot it.

We feed our horses round bales free choice. That is, they have at least one bale in their pasture at all times. If we are expecting a storm or cold weather, we quickly add another two bales. Just in case. The horses also use them as a windbreak. We don't like to be caught unprepared by a blizzard without adequate feed!

The goats and sheep don't do well with free-choice round bales as they climb on them and waste quite a bit of hay. (Goats are picky eaters and won't eat hay that has manure and urine tracked on it—even if they were the ones that tracked it in.)

Instead of giving them free-choice round bales, we back close to the front of our goat barn and the pens, and gently drop the bale on its end. By cutting the twines and removing them, we can peel the cap off to go onto the compost pile. Then the good hay underneath can be unpeeled a little at a time with a pitchfork and fed to the sheep and goats.

Again, if you dump the hay into the pen, they will eat quite a bit and then leave the "dirty" hay. This is not only wasteful, but can be unhealthy as they can spread internal parasites among themselves. Not only are minute bits of manure tracked onto the hay unappetizing, but they may contain worm eggs.

We have made our outside pens from welded livestock panels fastened to steel fence posts. We feed our hay just outside this fence, letting the animals reach through the squares in the fence to eat. They seldom pull hay into the pen and there is little chance of manure getting into the hay. We save money, clean pens less often, and have healthier animals. Can you ask for more?

As we feed the hay, sooner or later it becomes hard to unwind as the hay toward the bottom becomes wedged under the edge of the bale. At this point, we tip the bale over, away from the hay we can't work out. This leaves a large layer of hay on the ground to feed up, as well as the nice fat, but manageable core of the bale.

The water system

Before freezing weather had come upon us, we had a crew install a septic system and also bury a water line from our well to the basement, with a T toward the goat barn. At the end of this T, a frost-free hydrant was installed. And right next to the hydrant, we moved our handy-dandy fish house. When we had first moved to the homestead, we temporarily attached this 8'x12' building to our travel trailer, using it as a living room and a place for a propane wall furnace. (Without electricity, you can't run a travel trailer furnace; there is no way to use the fan.)

But after we moved out of the travel trailer (and mobile home), we didn't need the fish house. We figured it would make a terrific generator shed. So, planning ahead, we had the wiring for the pump also buried in the 8'-deep trench from the well, up the side trench by the frost-free hydrant, coming out of the ground a few feet from the spot the generator shed would be.

Without grid power, we (at present) depend on intermittent generator power. So using "normal" household plumbing for our water system would not work. It isn't feasible to keep turning on the generator every time the water pressure in a pressure tank gets low.

Instead, we installed a 350-gallon poly water tank in the basement and my oldest son, Bill, plumbed in a variable-speed 12-volt water pump. Bill works with an RV dealer and is very familiar with year-round upscale RV living options.

So our system works like this: When we want to fill the poly storage tank, which is about once every 10 days, we turn on the faucet in the basement where the water line comes into the house from the well. At present, we have a water hose connected to it, running overhead to the tank. We turn on the generator and throw the switch for the well, and the tank fills.

At the bottom of the tank, a flexible line runs to the 12-volt pump mounted to the concrete block basement wall, then on to the toilets, and just lately, a tap near the kitchen sink. When you flush the toilet, the pump quickly fills the tank. It also provides good water pressure in the kitchen, where I have a short length of hose to fill the canning kettle I heat water with. When you shut off the tap, the pump stops. Pretty neat.

The pump is wired to a deep-cycle battery connected to a charge controller. This charges the battery while the generator is running and also keeps it from overcharging. After living a long time without running water, this is a minor miracle to me!

In fact, when Bill hooked up my toilet, we stood around and had a flushing party when the first flush took place. My ever-economical sister, Sue, complained, though: "And I had to pee! You wasted all that water!"

With running water, flushing toilets, a warm house, and all that room, I feel so blessed.

As with everything here on our low-budget homestead, any and all large purchases must be planned for in advance. For instance, one month we bought two toilets and their plumbing. As Mom is in a wheel-chair and Dad (94) is using a walker, we installed a toilet right next to their bed for ease of use, especially at night. The second is a "normal" toilet, although with a handicapped accessible stool, in our large bath-room.

So far, we had been taking baths by heating up four canning kettles to very hot on the stove, carrying them to the tub, then carrying enough cold water from the faucet in the kitchen to make a nice hot bath. Showers are accomplished by using a battery-operated, handheld shower-er with the strainer being placed in a canning kettle of hot water on the floor. It does the job, but we wanted a powerful shower. I can pee hard-er than the battery shower puts out.

Our next expense was a propane water heater. I shopped around and found basically the same unit for $290 (Menards in Duluth) and $600 at our local gas compa-ny. So I asked my son, Bill, if he could pick up a tank the next time he was coming up this way.

He got the tank and enough double-insulat-ed B vent pipe to go up through Mom and Dad's closet corner and out through the

Me in the "mini pantry" in the entryway to the basement stairs

115

north roof of the house. When he and David hauled the tank into the basement, I could actually feel that forthcoming pounding hot shower.

But the next night, David and I opened the faucet in the basement to fill the big poly tank and water the goats from the outside frost-free hydrant. I stood in the generator shed to throw the switch for the submersible pump in the well and popped it up. Nothing happened! We had had 20-below temperatures, and our water line had frozen.

Talk about a sinking feeling. I knew we shouldn't be driving over our water line, even though it is buried eight feet in the ground. And I knew I should heap straw over the steel well casing. But, somehow I shrugged it off and hoped it would be all right. Wrong.

Hoping for the best, we dropped a trouble light with a caged 100-watt light bulb down the casing on an extension cord. (Maybe the line was frozen where the pitless adapter goes out through the casing to the water line. Elbows *do* freeze first…) But, we only run the generator in the evenings, and so far it hasn't worked.

Okay, we like the flush toilets and the convenience of a tap to draw water for dishwater. But, how could we haul water from the spring and fill the 350 poly tank so we could continue our present state of "civilization?" I pondered that all night and had an idea. I would buy three of those rolling garbage containers on wheels. We could bucket water in 5-gallon pails from the spring, fill the garbage cans, then back up to our ramp. With the tailgate dropped down, they would slide right off and we could roll them into the kitchen.

Luckily, we had installed a large floor grate in the kitchen, only a few feet away from the poly tank in the basement, so the warmth from the propane floor heater in the basement would radiate up into the living space.

So, David and I gave it a try. And it worked very well. With the big tank one third full, we hauled two loads of water in our three new garbage cans, filling the tank nearly full. From the kitchen grate, David would poke up the end of the garden hose we had previously filled the tank from, from the well. I stuck it into the water, and he would give a few good sucks on the other end to start the siphon. Then he stuck it into the big tank, letting the water flow. Each garbage can brought home 30 gallons (they were actually 35-gallon cans, but we slop out about 5 gallons on our rough roads).

As one can was almost empty, I would quickly kink the hose and transfer it to another can. It went very quickly and let us continue flushing until spring melts the frost out of our water line. (We kept the light down the well casing, just in case.)

In the spring, we will clear a good parking area and turn-around spot so we will not be driving on our water line next winter, and David will not plow the area above it, as he is doing now. The snow will act as insulation, and the vehicles will not compact the soil, driving frost deeper into the ground. And I will be sure to insulate the casing head where it sticks up out of the ground.

Most folks don't have this much trouble with a water line buried that deep, but because we live off-grid and run water through the line much less often than "normal," it's easier for it to freeze. And it's **never** a good idea to drive regularly over a water line.

Of course, I knew this and did not listen to *"Ask Jackie!"* Live and learn. Or at least learn to listen to my inner voice.

The generator shed

When you live in cold country, off-grid, you need to make provisions for the generator for winter. First, the generator needs some type of shelter to keep ice and snow off it when it's not being used. And second, generators don't start well (or hardly at all) when temperatures go below zero. Last winter, we had limped along by framing the generator on three sides with plywood and tarping the other side when it was not in use. But this was Mickey Mouse, to say the least. It resulted in the generator being frozen in the spot for weeks because the engine heated the snow, melting it into a deep puddle beneath the generator. This quickly froze once the generator was turned off. Not very ideal.

So early this winter, with our carpenter Tom's help, we dragged/carried the fish house down by the goat pen and frost-free hydrant. After leveling it and temporarily blocking it up, Tom installed a used breaker box on one wall and, later, a propane wall heater we had previously used when we used the shed as a living room.

Now, we keep the pilot only on the heater, and an hour before we want to run the generator, we simply turn up the heat. By the time we are ready to run the generator, it is warmed up toasty warm and starts on two or three pulls. This is compared to 15 or 20 hard pulls when the engine is cold and the oil is thick. To keep the generator from choking out from lack of oxygen, we open the south-facing window a few inches. Then we turn the flame down to pilot on the heater because the generator produces a lot of heat.

To make things more interesting, when it goes below about -15 degrees, the vehicles don't start. Here in Minnesota, as in other cold climates, most vehicles have a plug-in engine block heater. This effectively warms up the oil, making the vehicle start easily. Of course, we can't leave a vehicle plugged in overnight, which is the "norm." We don't run the generator that long; who could afford to?

So our system is this: Say David must leave for the bus at 6:30 am. I rise at 3 am and turn up the flame on the heater in the generator shed. By 4:30, the generator is toasty, right to its heart. I start the generator with the truck previously being plugged in (so I don't have to fool around at zero dark thirty when it's cold outside). By the time the alarm rings at 6 am, the truck is warmed up enough that it starts with little complaint. A bit complicated, but we usually only have to do this a few times during a winter.

Usually, we can just wait a few hours in the morning and the temperatures warm up to zero or above, and the vehicles start.

Throughout the winter, we have continued to work on the interior of the house. Our projects have included putting the log siding on the upstairs gable ends of David's and my bedrooms, staining that, finishing off the closet and painting the walls in Mom and Dad's bedroom, installing a tub/shower in the bathroom, and hooking up lighting fixtures in all the rooms. We have kept busy.

And throughout all, David has done a very good job plowing our mile-plus-long trail with the Ford F250 4x4 we bought from Bill (to replace the old, very dead Jeep we used last year). The Jeep was cheaper, but Bill's Ford is 100 times the truck. The plow is, too, being an old commercial plow that angles and throws the snow far off the trail.

We did have our problems, though. One night, David got off the bus and jumped into the truck to warm it up to plow going home. He raised the plow to leave (you should never park a truck with a snowplow on it with the plow up; it's hard on the hydraulics and springs), the lights dimmed seriously. Then when he got home, the truck killed when he tried to raise the plow. Just instantly went dead.

Instantly, I imagined all the horrible (and expensive) repairs that could be necessary. But, David called Bill and he told him to clean up the battery terminals, then retighten them. I helped him do this, and miracle of miracles, the truck instantly started and the plow groaned and   raised
normally.

A few nights later, the plow simply wouldn't raise at all, but the lights stayed on, and the truck ran fine. Another phone call to Bill (who is an automotive diagnostic technician, by the way), and he walked us through the checkups. No taillights? Check the fuse. Yep, the fuse was blown. We were back in business.

The next night, the taillights were bright, the truck ran, but the plow wouldn't raise or even groan. Yet another call. (Bill must be getting sick of hearing from us, by now. Love ya' Bill!) We again ran through the check list, and it produced no results. Finally, David put jumper cables from the battery to the plow motor, and I tapped the motor housing smartly with a hammer, and it came to life. The brushes had just been stuck with a bit of ice. Back in business.

Our friend, Tom Richardson,
working on the new green room floor

Now we are much smarter about the truck and plow. This is about how I learned to sweatsolder water pipes. My pipes had frozen when Bill was in diapers, and I called Dad. Over the phone 700 miles away, Dad talked me through repairing my pipes. You can learn just about anything with a good teacher.

Our new greenhouse

Well, it's March now, and I've already got some tomatoes and peppers poking up, nice and green in our kitchen window. But even that south-facing window doesn't provide enough light to keep them happy. They started leaning, looking for the sun, just about as soon as they had germinated. I bought a four-foot shop light and hung that about six inches above them. Just about instantly, they looked happier. (You don't need a gro-light to raise plants. I'm sure they are better, but I can't afford one.)

But I know how fast tomatoes grow, and we needed to meet their needs real soon. Last spring, we had built a 10'x10' greenhouse onto the mobile home. This was excellent, but it's still there, and we are here. It would be very difficult to heat that enough for growing plants while we are living down here. What to do? Put up a Mickey Mouse temporary greenhouse somewhere? Try to use the one at the mobile? We had to do something.

So, finally, we decided to build a green room attached to the south side of the new house. Tom came last Saturday, and we put up temporary treated 4'x4' corner posts, then framed the 10'x16' deck with treated 2"x8"s, then he and David quickly took the corrugated clear fiberglass down off the roof of the old greenhouse while I carried pots, planters, and other equipment out of the greenhouse.

This week, we'd like to switch the decking and begin framing the temporary roof, using the old corrugated fiberglass. We plan on putting an insulated roof over the green room, with a skylight over the living room window, then running a porch the entire length of the south side of the house. So we will use the deck, which will be permanent, but later remove the fiberglass roofing and rafters when we build the porch and roof the entire house.

By doing this, I can grow lots of plants for the garden this spring, then refinish the greenhouse for a permanent green room to allow me to grow vegetables year-round. I don't like buying out-of-season vegetables from Mexico and Chile! They still use pesticides banned (but still manufactured, by the way) in the U.S. that have been proven to be deadly additions to your diet. And besides, I refuse to pay $3 for a tomato or fresh sweet red bell pepper.

I have grown many vegetables indoors on a sun porch during the winter. I even had a nice dwarf peach tree that bore lots of gorgeous peaches down in Sturgeon Lake, Minnesota, 20 years back. So I know it can be done, and it will make us even more self-reliant down the pike.

It is a bit frustrating to sock every nickel into the house and homestead. Even grabbing a burger at a fast food joint is sometimes out of the question; I buy nails instead. But the light is getting brighter at the end of the tunnel. So I snatch up my nails and run for the light. ✍

Chapter Ten

Spring is here! Glorious spring is here, and our water line thawed out! After being without running water from our well to our basement storage tank and the frost-free hydrant by the goat barn, we had thawing. Our snow went very early this year. It's been gone for over a month and the frost followed by only two weeks, but our deep-in-the-ground water line took an extra two weeks after the frost had gone to thaw out. I had been trying the well switch every day for a few seconds and always the same; nothing but a hum as the pump kicked on way down in the well. But on April 22, our carpenter friend, Tom Richardson, showed up and was getting ready to work on the new green room addition to the house. As he would be cutting lumber with a circular saw, I went out to the generator shed and started the generator. Out of habit and wishful thinking, I flipped up the pump switch, glancing out the window to the open frost-free hydrant. Water began flowing happily out of the spout.

I ran out into the driveway and yelled for David and Tom. (I think they figured I'd finally gone off the deep end.) Then we all chatted happily, watching the hose fill up the goat water tank. It was so good to watch that clear water flow. Of course, we then quickly topped off the 350 gallon poly storage tank in the basement of the house and all had a good drink of ice water from the hose. Not wanting it to stop, I also connected the hose to the horse watering tank down in the pasture and filled that, as well. For me, it was a major miracle. (And a reminder not to drive on the water line this winter and to thoroughly insulate the steel well casing that sticks up out of the ground.)

The greenhouse emerges

Our first spring project was to get the temporary greenhouse built onto the south side of the new log house. I desperately needed it done so I could transplant my spindly tomato and pepper plants from inside the house. Although I had installed a four-foot shop light to give them more light than a kitchen window would provide, we simply did not run the generator long enough to give the plants as much light as they craved. We had torn down the old greenhouse from the mobile home, and Tom refit it to the larger dimensions available on the new house. Where it had been 10'x10', now it is 10'x16'. It took one Saturday afternoon to deck the surface, using screws and the treated 5/4 decking. There was a lot of cutting to fit so that we didn't waste any material. (Tom is great at that. We only ended up with a few waste scraps too small to reuse.)

The floor was screwed down to treated 2x8s, which were hung in rafter hangers for extra support. As this will be a permanent deck, but

The new "temporary" greenhouse

built on temporary pillars, we got it as level as possible with the snow still going off. In the future, we will be using used power poles for porch supports and rafters, as the green room and porch will extend across the full south side of the house.

Eventually, the green room will have insulated windows (reject double-pane patio doors Tom salvaged from another job), along with insulation in the roof, and crawl space underneath. So we are making another "temporary" greenhouse to get by with until it gets rebuilt, this time for the last time.

The reason we are going "temporary" now is that we still have the silver tarps on the roof and can't take the time to place the heavy pole rafters and supports for the finished roof; the temporary roof is the corrugated fiberglass paneling from the old greenhouse, hung on 2x6 rafters with 2x4 purlins, installed under the house roof to shed water easily.

After decking the greenhouse, the next Saturday afternoon was spent hanging rafters, screwing down purlins and the thin corrugated wooden support strips for the lightweight roofing, then screwing down the roofing. As the old roofing was longer than the roofing we needed, Tom reversed a blade in his circular saw and we were able to easily cut two pieces of roofing at a time. Nice and smooth. I had visions of splitting fiberglass flying around everywhere, but it cut very nicely.

I cut the panels and handed them up through the rafters to Tom and David, who were positioning them and screwing them down. There are a few holes that didn't line up, and leak when it rains, but I am going up there and filling them with dabs of silicone sealer. That does a great job and lasts for years.

Before it was very late, Tom managed to frame and hang a few of the old windows on the south side (also leftovers from other jobs). It looked pretty darned good. Then on Sunday afternoon, David and I went to work and hung more windows on the east and west ends of the greenhouse. Two of these were windows that opened, having screens for ventilation on hot days. Then we screwed blocks over the openings at the eaves and finished up by hanging doubled 6-mil plastic over the odds and ends openings that we had no windows to fit. Not gorgeous, but certainly functional.

The very next day, we moved the homemade tables and benches down from the mobile home and installed them in the new greenhouse. Finishing up with a large dollar store thermometer, we moved the plants into their new home.

Of course, although the daytime temperatures out there were in the 70s, the night temperatures fluctuated down into the 20s without heat. So I carefully carried in the plants each evening, just to make sure none froze after all that work.

But, those sorry plants sure needed help; they were so leggy. So, I went to work and began transplanting. I've found that my plants do best when transplanted into large Styrofoam cups (also dollar store). I set to work filling them with potting soil, then

Hundreds of transplanted tomato and pepper plants thrive in the greenhouse.

burying them so that only the strong, straight top showed at the top. Tomatoes will grow roots all along the buried stem, making the leggy plants stronger, and peppers don't mind a bit being planted deeply.

I used a tablespoon for a transplanting trowel, carefully handling the plants only by the leaves. You can easily damage the stem of the young plant by squeezing it with your fingers. This can even kill the plant. Even if you pull off a leaf, no lasting damage is done.

The only problem with using the Styrofoam cups is that they are tippy when full. To solve this problem, I cut down cardboard banana boxes that I get goat scraps in from our local supermarket. These boxes are heavy and have handles on the ends, which I carefully leave. The only problem is that the boxes have a large ventilation hole in the bottom. To solve this, I simply cut strips of leftover cardboard to lay over the holes.

Then, as I transplanted, I put each cup into the box, filling it snugly. When I have to move a box of plants, it is simple and safe to do. (And I'm glad to find another use for those boxes.)

When I finished, I had more than 100 tomato plants of 13 varieties. I was amazed, as I thought I was a little short of tomatoes. Of course, I'll give some to my son Bill and his wife, a few to Tom, the carpenter, and trade a few with friends for a few different varieties. And I came out with about 60 peppers of seven different kinds.

Two weeks later, every single one of those plants is thriving and getting very strong and lusty. They love their new home. I can't wait to get them moved out into the garden in their snug Wallo' Waters. The temperatures are okay now, lows getting only into the mid 20s, but I don't have the garden ready yet.

Mom and Dad have both had hospital stays in April due to the flu and pneumonia, so I was more than a little busy and couldn't garden when I wanted to.

Canning pork loin and chicken breast

But while I had to be in the house more than I wanted, it did give me time to stock up on my meat. Our local supermarket was selling some very good whole boneless pork loin and chicken breasts at a huge savings, so I bought as much as I thought I could handle canning.

These were very easy to can. I simply boiled a batch of breasts or a cut-in-half pork loin, with seasoned water, in a very large stock pot until the meat was about half cooked. This let it shrink and become firm enough to cut if needed and fit nicely into the jars. I packed the chicken breasts whole into wide-mouth pint jars. Leftover pieces, I diced into half pints. Then the jars were filled to within an inch of the top of the jars with the hot broth they were boiled in.

I processed the hot-packed chicken at 10 pounds pressure in my pressure canner, in pints and half-pints for 75 minutes, and it turned out absolutely wonderful.

The pork loin was sliced or diced, depending on the part of the loin I was working with. The nicest meat was simply sliced about half an inch thick and slid carefully into pint and quart jars. Some was diced and packed into pint jars to use for casseroles and barbecue pork. All was covered with the hot broth that the meat was boiled in, to within an inch of the top of the jars.

This was canned in a pressure canner at 10 pounds pressure for 75 minutes (pints) and 90 minutes (quarts).

I put up 12 pounds of boneless chicken breasts and three whole boneless pork loins in two afternoons, giving us meat for more than 56 meals. Well worth the effort, I'd say.

During Mom and Dad's recovery at the hospital, I also had my bi-monthly x-rays and lab work to make sure my cancer was gone. It's been a year since I began treatment for the pea-sized lump on my elbow, which turned out to be a rare Merkel Cell Carcinoma, and I am very happy to report that everything came back absolutely normal.

Getting the garden ready

Now, with all those plants growing so nicely in the greenhouse, it was time for me to get busy and get the garden ready to go. And with the weather being so fantastic for the time of year, I wanted to get some of the earliest crops in, like peas, carrots, turnips, onions, and lettuce. Because my oldest son, Bill, had vastly enlarged the garden with his crawler last summer, removing many tree stumps, logs, and large rocks, the whole thing needed lots of work to get ready for planting.

I had planned to get my large hoop house up this spring, but because of Mom and Dad's illnesses, that just won't happen. I'll use other methods of protecting my tender crops until next year.

Because my large garden is on a gentle slope next to the house, it is basically a slope of gravel and rock—not the best soil, but it's what we've got. Last fall, David hauled the compost pile (rotted goat and chicken manure and straw) onto the garden with our little Ford tractor and loader. It was spread quite well, but there were still humps and piles here and there. And brush roots. Oh my.

As the garden now measures about 100'x100', there's lots of fixin' that needs to be done. David brought the garden trailer down to the garden with his ATV, and we picked rocks all afternoon. Then I tilled, unearthing many more. So while David picked those rocks, I began to pick up, pull up, and dig up tree and brush roots. Some of them were 10 feet long. And if I had not pulled them, they would have suckered little sprouts all over the garden.

David picks up rocks in the big garden.

I'm very sure we didn't get all the big rocks or roots. But this is an ongoing process, and we will be at it for years. Our garden in Montana was also carved out of virgin slope under like conditions. And when we left, it was a pretty darned good piece of ground. It is amazing at how much improvement a lot of work and rotted manure can make on a less than perfect garden. The trick in all gardening is perseverance. If you quit or "put up with bad conditions," you lose.

Once we got the upper side of the garden worked up quite well, I hooked our furrowing attachment onto the Troy-Bilt. I had found a terrific sale on two-year-old, very large roots of Jersey Giant asparagus. All of the Jersey asparagus varieties are pretty much "all-male" plants. The female asparagus plants are the ones that produce the little red berries. And they are generally less productive as table asparagus, as they put much of their energy into reproduction. With the all-male hybrids, you get bigger, fatter, and more asparagus. Last year I planted a dozen Mary Washington (plain, common garden asparagus) down on the edges of our paths, as tame "wild" asparagus. It's growing, but I wanted more asparagus and easier access to the kitchen. As asparagus is one of our favorite crops, I bought two packs of 10 roots each. (We ended up with three "free" roots, to boot.)

Planting asparagus is a bit different than many crops. The best way is to dig a trench along the row, about 8" to 10" deep. Spreading the roots out as much as possible, I laid the roots into the trench about a foot and a half apart. I have a pile of two-year-old, very black rotted compost that I forked onto the plants, covering each one by about two inches of the compost. Then, in between the plants, I forked some of the year-old rotted manure to provide fertilizer and keep down any sprouting weeds.

As the asparagus grows, I'll keep covering it, just like you'd do hilling potatoes. This buries the roots deeply, but encourages plant growth.

On the near end of each trench, I planted rhubarb that I transplanted from the gravel slope. It wasn't getting enough water or care, and I know that it'll be much happier down in the main garden, especially since I dug in several forkfuls of well-rotted manure around each plant.

I like as many perennial plants around the place as possible. They just keep getting better each and every year. Rhubarb and strawberries yield

My on-sale asparagus roots were huge. I spread the roots to place in the furrows, then place the asparagus roots in the trench. After covering the plants with black compost, I fill in between with one-year-old rotted manure.

the first tame fruit on a new homestead, so are much cherished. But I have also planted "slower" fruits.

Two years ago, my parents and sister gave me five apple trees (Haralson and Haralred) for my birthday, and we planted these in what will eventually be our orchard/chicken yard. Last year, I planted a hardy pie cherry, a Minnesota apricot (Moonglow), a Honeycrisp and Fireside apple, along with Manchurian apricots and Nanking cherries, a hardy bush cherry.

On checking my baby trees this spring, I've (maybe) lost only one apple tree. Everything else is popping out leaves and even a few flowers. David and I just planted an Alderman plum, which is now flowering. But on the littlest trees, I'll pinch the blossoms off so the trees will put all their energy into growing and developing strong roots. It's hard, but will pay in the long run.

I was worried about the trees I planted last spring. Because of all the running to the hospital, I didn't get the trunks covered with screen or fencing around the trees. Voles, mice, and rabbits will girdle the lower trunk of young trees, often right under the snow. This nearly always kills the trees. I had it happen years ago with more than 20 young apple trees, so I learned my hard lesson. And deer love to munch on the twigs, bark, and upper branches of the sweet young trees. I lucked out. The trees sailed through the winter without becoming lunch for our wild neighbors.

With all the newly planted fruit, which should begin bearing a little this year or next, we also have so much wild fruit around: Red raspberries, blueberries, chokecherries, and wild plums. I feel blessed. My new basement pantry is all ready to receive this summer's bounty.

Disbudding our baby goats' horns

We had two single goat births on the homestead, earlier this spring. They were both very nice baby bucks. We raise Nubian-Boer crossbreds. The Nubians are colorful, elegant big milkers with cute, floppy big ears. But they tend to be like race horses, tall and narrow. We wanted more size and meat ability, so for years we have been crossing Nubians with Boer meat goats and have been happy with the results. The does milk about three quarts to more than a gallon a day of very good tasting milk. And the bucks and wethers are very large and quickly put on bulk. Chevon (goat meat) is very good, being consumed worldwide, much more than is beef. And when you have limited refrigeration and no freezer, you can handle the meat that comes off a goat, where 800 pounds of beef is just too much to handle in many cases.

All of my goats are hornless. They were not born that way, but were disbudded soon after birth. No, that is not what nature intended, but nature didn't intend that goats be penned up and milked twice a day. Horns on goats may be "protection," but I have seen our old hornless Nubian doe run a big coyote all the way across our acre of pasture. Goats have a big attitude and don't generally have predator trouble, unless they are on a tether chain and stake or in a small pen. Then it is usually a dog that will be the culprit, rather than a wild animal.

Horns are just trouble on a homestead goat. They get stuck in fences, mangers, and ropes, even their own collars, sometimes resulting in strangulation and death. Does sometimes break the legs of their own kids by butting at them and catching a kid's leg in the V between the horns. And the horns are a definite danger to the person handling and milking them. Goats don't mean to hurt you with them, but by turning their head quickly, they can bang your face, twist your fingers, and otherwise do harm, especially to children who are not so observant and careful when handling them.

It's a major surgery to remove the horns from an adult goat, but very easy to do with kids. At about three days of age, we disbud them. This involves using an electric disbudding iron, available at most goat supply houses for around $50. I heat the iron to coppery red, then while David holds the kid on his lap securely, I apply the hot iron to first one horn bud, rocking it slowly in a circular motion for even disbudding, then the other bud. I hold the iron on each horn bud for about seven seconds; just enough to burn a good even light-colored ring completely around each horn.

Then I go back and see if the edge of the iron will flip off the burned scab on the tip of the bud. It usually does, and I repeat the process on each one, for a little less time. Yes, the kid does yell, but not as much as you'd think. And then it's over.

I apply a handful of snow on each bud, then give the kid a bottle or let it back in with its mother. It happily drinks and seems to forget all about the process. They don't fear you and don't seem to feel in pain. And you have just saved their life or prevented injury to a person you love. I don't like doing it. It stinks of burning hair, and I hate to hear the kids bawl. But it really is necessary. If you can't afford an iron, go into partnership with a friend and help each other disbud. It goes easier with two people, anyway.

But, you can do it alone. Build a kid holding box. This is a narrow plywood box, just wide enough for the kid's standing body to fit in. The top is hinged at the back and there's a notch in the front just big enough to let his head and neck stick out. There is a small, semi-circular shelf just below the notch for his chin to rest on. So once in, the kid can't move around much. You can sit on the box and hold his head down with one hand and use the disbudding iron with the other. It goes quite nicely this way. You can make a box yourself or buy one.

A goat supply house that I use a lot for everything from disbudding irons to cheese making supplies is Hoegger Supply Company, P.O. Box 331, Fayetteville, Georgia 30214 or www.thegoatstore.com.

Planting wildflowers

As spring is here full-force, many of the daffodil, crocus, and grape hyacinth bulbs that I planted last fall and the year before are popping up and blooming. It's always such a thrill when the first cheerful crocus opens and sings to the morning sun.

I like to bring beauty everywhere, so I am constantly planting bulbs and flowers, often in unexpected places. Right now, Bob's memorial garden is coming alive with flowers and birdsong. Besides the flowers, I have bird feeders and houses in several places, so the mornings ring with song. (And the birds also help keep the insect pests out of my garden, so attracting them serves a two-fold purpose.)

Of course, we have many wildflowers here on the homestead, but I always pop in a few more. It seems that I can't get enough flowers; I like something blooming all the time. It encourages your soul.

I'm planting daylilies (you can also eat daylily buds), which come back every year, bigger and stronger, requiring minimal care. And I'm planting lots of wildflower seeds in the disturbed area around our building site. One spot, especially, cried out for help. That is the large denuded area where the septic drain field lies. Major ugly. So I ordered inexpensive wildflower seeds from Wildseed Farms, 425 Wildflower Hills, P.O. Box 3000, Fredricksburg, Texas 78624-3000 or www.wildseedfarms.com. With a crank-type seeder, I mixed fine seed-starting medium with the mixed seeds and walked back and forth on the bare, loose soil. It had been raining, so the soil was just waiting for the seeds.

Then, after the seeds were spread evenly, I gently ran the ATV back and forth on the area, packing the seeds into the damp ground. A more accepted way is to gently till the soil an inch deep, then seed, then roll the area or walk on it to press the seeds into the ground. But on our gravel pit soil, that would be about impossible without major work. I'm sure that unorthodox method will work fine.

Luckily it will rain off and on all week. But I have a hose and sprinkler out there if it should stop. New seeds must be kept damp (not soggy) while germinating and beginning to grow. That ugly spot will soon be a glowing haven for hummingbirds and butterflies—not to mention me. ᔥ

Chapter Eleven

$\mathcal{I}$'m looking out the upstairs bedroom window where my desk is. The green is *so* intense. The poplar trees are in full leaf now and their bright, shiny green contrasts with the darker green of the pine and balsam, dancing with the soft blue green of the white spruce. The beaver ponds are dark, reflecting the woods around them. Somewhere to the west, a loon cries its weird laugh as it flies to one of the dozens of lakes in the area. Welcome, summer in the north woods.

I needed an evening like tonight. Last week we lost Dad, 94, who lived at home with us. After a long bout with recurrent pneumonia and being in the hospital for two weeks, he just stopped breathing. Just three weeks ago, he'd been laughing and enjoying the day as my son, Bill, came up bringing a battery-powered golf cart, giving Mom and Dad rides all around the homestead. Dad had a hard time walking with a walker and Mom is in a wheelchair, so neither of them get around outside as much as they'd like. Both enjoyed their rides very much. I try to remember that day, and many, many in the past that we shared. But, it's hard, especially after losing my husband of 14 years, Bob, just a year and a half ago.

The garden

In the middle of May, we finally got the garden worked up and most of the serious rocks and roots picked out. So, we began to put in the garden. I laugh when people tell me they planted their garden "yesterday." It takes me weeks.

First to go in are the cold-weather crops. These are crops that not only

135

The tomatoes are ready to leave the greenhouse.

survive a freeze or frost, but seem to like this kind of weather. Because my pantry has gotten too low for my liking, I wanted a large enough garden so I could seriously restock it this summer and fall. But, because it's a new garden, carved out of a patch of small trees and heavy brush, I couldn't make it as large as I would have liked this spring. It's about 50'x75', with room to enlarge it (with lots of work) to double that size in the future. But, this year's garden is still much smaller than I really need to grow everything I want to. Therefore, I had to be creative in laying out things.

First to go in were the onions and carrots. I planted the onions in a three-foot-wide bed, placing the onion sets three inches apart all ways. In the same space that I could have planted 50 sets in a single row, I planted 200 sets. On the end of the onion bed went the carrots. But, like the onions, I needed more carrots than one row would allow...and all I had room for was that one row. So I planted a 20-foot row, placing a light planting of radishes in the row to mark it and also make it a double row; two crops grown in one row. Then, I moved over four inches and planted another row of carrots, giving me two rows in a little more space than one row took. (Carrots also do well in a wide-bed planting, but our soil is just too rough yet. In a year or two, I'll plant even more carrots in a smaller space, using a well-worked wide bed.)

After the carrots and onions were in, I planted two 40-foot rows of Yukon Gold potatoes, then a 20-foot row of a potato my grandfather grew in the Gallatin Valley of Montana called Bliss Triumph. This is a solid, white-meat red potato that is very good for all uses and stores

136

well into the spring. I planted another 20 foot row of Ozette, a fingerling potato grown by Native Americans in the northwest. I grew it by accident back when we lived on the farm in Sturgeon Lake, Minnesota, and I'll always remember how much we loved its taste and unique (almost waxy) texture.

Between the Yukon Gold and other potatoes, I left a spot for a row of bush beans. I was planning on planting a row of Provider bush beans and want to save seed for next year. Beans should have 20 feet or more between varieties to avoid cross-pollination when you save seed. That spot was perfect.

But it was too early to plant beans; we were expecting at least a couple of frosts before the weather settled to safer spring-like weather. Instead, I planted squash, pumpkin, melons, watermelon, and cucumber seeds in Styrofoam cups in the greenhouse. I can get a big jump on these crops by starting plants inside and transplanting them when the soil warms up. Not only do I gain a month of growing season for these longer-season crops, but the plants can be gently set out in warm weather, and they take off like shooting stars. I plant these only four or five weeks ahead of the time I want to set them out. If the vines get too large, the plants never seem to do well in the garden.

I also planted cabbage, broccoli, and cauliflower plants that we had grown in the new greenhouse.

And I set out 34 tomato and 22 pepper plants, a dozen at a time. Wait! Too early to plant beans, but I'm setting out tomatoes and peppers? Hah! I planted them in my gardening partners, Wallo' Waters. I had experienced 18° F weather for several nights, with a foot of new snow, back in

End of week one: All tomatoes and peppers are planted.

137

*Mom and Bill enjoy
the garden.*

Montana, and knew for a fact that not only do these little plastic tipis protect the plants, but actually make them thrive and grow quickly into stocky, well-rooted plants.

So my son, David, and I took turns filling the cells of the Wallo' Waters with water. (It is a little hard on your back after a few.) We would set the plant in deeply, then place a five-gallon bucket over it, upside down. Then the Wallo' Water would go on. One of us sat on another upside down bucket and held each cell open to receive the garden hose and the other would stand and place the running hose into each cell. This way, the tomatoes went in quite quickly. (All except the night that David was away. I turned on the weather radio just before dark and was shocked to hear the "F" word: Frost warning! And I had planted a dozen tomatoes and a dozen peppers without the Wallo' Waters, figuring on doing it in the morning when I had help.)

I grabbed a flashlight, ran out and turned on garden hoses, then started the generator, switched on the pump, and ran down to the garden. I filled six Wallo' Waters before my back started screaming. But the moon had come out full and cold into a starry, clear sky. There was a definite chill in the air; frost was sure to come. I couldn't stop. So I squirmed around, filled plastic, got wet, cold, and miserable, but kept filling Walls. Finally there were only two plants left uncovered. I just couldn't bear to do another one, so I set the two buckets upside-down over each plant, figuring that would surely protect them.

I turned off the water and went in the house, shivering, to a hot bath.

In the morning, there was not only frost on everything, but ice a half an inch thick on the water tub for the goat pen. Ice!

When I later checked the garden, all the plants in the Wallo' Waters were fine and dandy. But, the two under the buckets were black and dead as a doornail.

Luckily, I had dozens of plants left in the greenhouse, so I pulled them up and replanted them, along with more the next day. (One of those plants was a Silvery Fir Tree tomato, and it started growing from the root, right in the edge of the onion bed, where I threw it. Now, five weeks later, it's nearly as tall as the plant I replaced it with. I don't have the heart to kill it, so it's growing with the onions).

By the time we got all the tomatoes and peppers planted, it was time to seed in the beans and corn. I planted seven fairly short (15') rows of sweet corn, each with 10 Tom Thumb popcorn seeds at the north end of the row, making two adjacent blocks of corn. Corn grows best in blocks of rows, instead of one or two long rows. This ensures complete pollination. If the ears are not pollinated well, they do not fill out to the tip or else fill out poorly all along the ear.

The reason that I can grow popcorn and sweet corn in the same garden right next to each other, is that the popcorn is an 85-day corn and the sweet corn is a 62-day corn. They will pollinate at different times, therefore ensuring that they don't cross. This crossing would make impure seed and might affect the taste of the sweet corn.

Corn requires a great deal of space between varieties when you are saving seed, and some types of sweet corn require isolation for the best taste. It is generally accepted that you need at least 200 feet between types of corn to keep relatively pure seed; a mile for truly pure seed.

If I'm in a hurry to get the corn to sprout, I'll soak it overnight in warm water, then plant it the next morning. This year, I was afraid of another frost, so I just planted it in the warm soil; we were having daytime temperatures in the 70s, so I knew it would come up well without soaking. (Never plant corn in cool soil. Let the soil warm up, even if it means waiting a week or more. Most corn seed does not germinate well in cold soil and will just sit there and rot.)

After the corn, I planted my bush green and yellow wax beans, then my three choices of pole beans for this year: Cherokee Trail of Tears, Brejo, and Chinese Red Noodle bean. I did not put the wire up for them to climb on yet. I prefer to do this just before the beans begin to climb so I can place it well.

By the time the beans were up, I figured we were about done with frost, so I pulled the Wallo' Waters off the first row of tomatoes. The tomatoes were already popping a foot out of the top. So, I pulled the protectors off carefully and staked the tomatoes. I will admit that when you first pull the Wallo' Waters off the plants, they look terrible; all long and floppy. But, I've learned that they have put down excellent roots, and with about 10 days of being staked, they look dramatically better.

I also planted a row of cukes, assorted squash, pumpkin, melon, and watermelon plants. The daytime temperatures were in the high 80s and with water, the garden was booming.

But that afternoon I noticed that the clouds were clearing off and the temperature was falling. No, no way! But I turned on the weather radio. It began with a frost warning. Oh crap.

Screaming for David, I headed for the garden, carrying all the tarps I

David and Tom sheathing roof. (Notice shirt stuffed in septic vent. Peeuee!)

could hold. He madly jumped on his four-wheeler and dashed for the mobile home, where we had another stash of tarps. Luckily, our friend Tom had pulled the huge tarp off of half of the house roof and begun to finish it so we had that tarp as well. For an hour, David, Tom, and I covered plants, being very careful not to mash them down. It looked like a war zone. But when the moon came up into a clear-as-a-bell sky, all but a short bit of one bush bean row was covered.

"Yeah, right," I grumped. "All that, and it probably won't freeze."

But it did. If we hadn't covered the garden, it would have frozen. The only thing we lost was that piece of uncovered bean row. And that was quickly replanted. You really need to pay attention to the weather here in the northland.

We removed the tarps and laid them all around the edges of the garden, just in case another freeze popped up. In addition, they would act as a deer barrier to help keep the pests out of the garden until we could take the time to get it fenced.

I spent time every day staking the tomatoes. The strongest, tallest stakes are on the indeterminate (vining) tomatoes. These continue to grow and grow, setting fruit until frost. But, I also stake my determinate tomatoes. These are shorter growing, stop growing, and set fruit. I stake them for protection against strong wind and breaking off when they are heavy with fruit.

To stake tomatoes, simply drive in a sharpened stake near the plant. I use everything from the 1"x1" stickers that held our sawmill lumber apart in the stacks, letting them air dry, to pipe and tomato cages from the dump. With soft yarn, strips of cloth, or anything that will not cut into the vines, I tie the plant to the stake. Usually, I begin tying at about a foot or so up the plant, and as the plant grows, I tie the main branches to the stake.

I found several part rolls of concrete reinforcing wire at the dump and brought them home to make tomato cages. This works very well, and the wide wire squares are easy to pick through. I just haven't had the time to make 'em yet. Oh well, maybe next year. It doesn't pay to get nuts about such things.

To make these cages, I unroll enough wire to make a cage about two

Tom is laying the starter row for shingles.

feet in diameter. Then, with bolt cutters or wire cutters, I cut off the wire, leaving long wires on my new cage. I roll the wire into a circle and use the wire ends to bend back, fastening the cage together securely. After this is done, I snip off the bottom wire, leaving all those sharp wires pointing downward. Then I go back and cut off three, leave one, cut off three, leave one, all around the circle. This leaves me with several sharp wires to push into the soil, holding the new tomato cage in place. This cage is set down over a lightly staked young plant. Then, as it grows, I reach my hand through the wire, guiding the growing vines out through the wire here and there.

Making tomato cages is a great winter project. I hope to use my toasty basement to manufacture many cages this year. (Last year I forgot to get the wire in, and it got buried in the deep snow. Now, where is that wire?) In the fall here in Minnesota, you'd better make sure all your tools are picked up or you won't see them until April. Snow sometimes comes early and stays late.

The house gets a roof

Well, half a roof, anyway.

Because our new log house is a pay-as-you-go building, I can afford to do only one project at a time. (You'll remember we spent last winter with no insulation in the roof and only two large construction-grade tarps on it, in place of roofing.) This did work very well and we were more than satisfied with the results. David's and my bedrooms are upstairs, and I'll admit that we had frost on the rafters and every nail head of the gable-end log siding when it was cold. Some nights it was cool in the bedrooms, but I can truthfully say I was never cold in bed; better than the place where we lived in New Mexico.

But, knowing that the tarps were not going to work as a long-term fix, I began saving money early in the year. Not trusting myself, I cashed my small income tax return check and handed it to Tom, in advance for the roofing job, then did the same with two more checks. Finally the weather was nice, and half of the house roof was paid for in advance. I like that; no worrying about paying for it later. (Sort of a reverse credit card purchase.)

So, one fine afternoon, Tom showed up with his huge red Ford truck, loaded down with scaffolding. And he began setting it up. I'm such a chicken about heights, I was glad he had strong planks to walk back and forth on the whole length of the house.

In the morning, the dogs started barking, and David and I stepped outside. A big truck was coming. Our roof was arriving. Sure, it was piles of lumber, Typar, boxes, and shingles, but it was our roof. How exciting! And it was going to be on before any serious rain came.

The following morning, Tom arrived in a cloud of dust and rapidly unloaded tools, safety harness, and rope for David, and our new roof was underway. Because I wanted the log rafters and beautiful knotty pine tongue-and-groove 2"x6" roof boards to show in the upstairs bedrooms, the insulation had to go outside, on top of the roof. And because we live in a climate that is pretty cold in the winter, Tom (a roofing specialist by trade as well as a fantastic cabinet maker) opted for a cold roof. This type of roof keeps the warmth in the house in the winter, yet lets cold air vent on top of the insulation, keeping condensation outdoors and not beading on the wood.

I was not familiar with this type of roof construction, so it was interesting to learn the whys and wherefores. Basically, this is how it went:

First David was fitted into a safety harness and roped to a fitting fastened to a log rafter. Then, he and Tom began tearing off the 1"x4" strips that held down our huge silver roof tarp. The day was warm, and that plastic tarp was slippery. Tom installed brackets and planks for ease of working, but they still had to be careful, especially at the edges of the roof where it dropped more than 25 feet.

After the tarp was down and folded up, Tom cut 2"x6"s to run from eave to the ridge peak, doubling them on the outside (leaving a small space between). Then, another 2"x6" was spiked on parallel to those, over two feet. This space was left uninsulated to keep the cold overhang cold and allow air to flow through it. Then, another 2"x6" was spiked horizontally from one vertical to the one on the opposite end of the house. This was to support the four inches of extruded foam insulation. Tom hauled out his hole saw and drilled a hole at either end in the vertical 2"x6" to let the cold air from the uninsulated roof over the overhang circulate into the spaces above the insulation. Then, 2"x6" blocks were cut from scrap lumber to support the horizontal 2"x6" firmly.

The stiff, light extruded foam board then went on. Quite a trick in the wind. I thought David was going to learn parasailing that day. After that was in place, 2"x4"s were laid, 16" on center, from the blocks at the eaves to the peak. These would hold the roof sheathing off the insulation board, allowing cool air to circulate over it, carrying off moisture.

On top of these, they nailed the OSB sheathing using long ringed pole barn nails, which went down through the OSB, the 2"x4"s, and the four inches of insulation board, anchoring firmly in the log rafters or 2"x6" roof boards.

Tom and David stretched a sheet of ice shield across the roof and stapled it down tightly. This is to protect the roof in case of ice dams, which can form on the eaves or valleys of a house from melting water trickling down to where it is colder and freezing. Subsequent melting can be forced uphill, under the shingles. The chances of this happening on our cold roof are very small, but we used the ice guard, just to be sure.

Once the first sheet was in place, the starting row of shingles was nailed in place. This is a narrow band of shingle material, cut with adhesive on both top and bottom side to ensure a tight seal. It went all along the bottom of the roof and along both ends.

Then our beautiful antique green shingles started going on. How exciting. (Of course it was even better because we had gotten a great deal on "last year's" shingles.) But, I really did like the color, and I liked it even better on our house.

After a few rows of shingles went on, another row of ice shield was stapled tightly in place, overlapping the one below. Then more shingles. When Tom got almost to the top of the row of ice shield, he stretched a roll of Typar underlayment, overlapping the row of ice shield, and stapled that tightly. Tom likes Typar better than tarpaper. It breathes better (less chance of condensation), it is tougher (less prone to ripping during installation), and it is lighter. In this manner, the rest of the roof was laid.

In one day, we went from ugly silver whale tarp to half the roof half shingled. It was amazing. Through all this, I acted as a gofer, handing up supplies, retrieving dropped nails, running to town for more nails, and so forth. Once the OSB was in place, Tom wanted no one on the roof with him. He said it was safer that way, with no one to watch out for. Seemed to work for him.

I was glad that Dad lived to see the finished roof go on. He was always asking how it was coming. Was Tom shingling yet? How did

Work on half the roof is half finished. Note roof brackets and planks for ease of working and safety.

145

it look? We brought him outside to see it the next morning, and he was extremely pleased with our new roof.

Now, I am in the process of saving for the south side of the roof. This is harder for me to wait for, after seeing how gorgeous the north side turned out. But the south side will be more expensive because we are putting in two six-foot dormers, one for each bedroom. Tom said he could do one dormer and half of the roof for one "job," and then do the other when I could afford it. Thanks, Tom.

Today he showed up unexpectedly, between jobs, and moved his scaffolding around to the west end of the house. I had saved enough to buy 200 lineal feet of 10" half-log siding, and tomorrow we will begin putting it up in the gable end (pointy end!) of the house. I'm doing the west end first, for that is the direction our bad weather usually comes from.

So, while he set up scaffolding, I hauled out a gallon of stain and began staining the house logs. I had planned to stain the log siding before it went up for ease of handling. But, my son, Bill, was out and suggested that I wait a couple of months to let the siding age. He said he'd done just what I had planned on doing, and the color didn't match his logs at all. They had weathered and the siding hadn't. (Yes, he

Bill taking Dad for a good ride around the homestead

cleaned and pressure washed his logs before staining, so the color was "new," but it didn't matter.) On the other end of his house he waited, and the color matched very well.

I guess I won't be staining the siding before I put it up. I'd rather learn from someone else's mistakes; I make enough of my own.

Somehow, I came up with a bum knee. For a while it was so painful that I could hardly walk. I was so glad that Bill left the little golf cart for me to take Mom around the place. For a while, it took *me* around the place. (By the way, I love that little rechargeable cart. No gas, no fumes, quiet, and it took me over the miles I walk every day.) Climbing ladders was definitely out, but today I managed to climb the pipe scaffolding and ungracefully clamber up onto the plank walkway. The knee is getting better, but I used an elastic knee brace, just to give it a little help.

One thing I've learned is to just keep going. No matter what. It's easy to fall into a pity bag when it seems like everything is smacking you in the face. But, if you can manage to put one foot in front of you (even if you have to use a golf cart) and keep going, things will work out. Just when I was pretty darned low, I got a nice letter in the mail, then David showed me a dozen electric green tree frogs taking a dip in our goats' watering trough one night. It's the little things like that, or seeing the first green tomatoes in the garden or the first tendrils on the cucumber vines. It brings a little smile to your soul and gives you the courage to go on. ♆

Chapter Twelve

How fast the summer has gone! Already the leaves are turning yellow on the popple trees around us. And just last night, I heard a big flock of geese honk by, right outside my upstairs bedroom window. I could hear the beat of their wings, they were so close. Beautiful, but telling me it's time to get ready for winter. As if that hasn't been happening all summer. Here in the northland, you begin getting ready for winter in May.

But we're so much more ready than we were last fall, when we were still living in that old mobile home, building on our log home every spare second. Where last fall we had only the ugly but serviceable silver construction tarp over our 2x6 roof boards (no insulation; couldn't afford it), we now have three-fourths of our house roofed and insulated. Because we pay as we go, our carpenter friend, Tom Richardson, has been doing our roofing by pieces. A bit peculiar, when most folks simply go to their bank and get a construction loan. But as our place is paid for, I do not want to get into debt. There are just too many things that can interfere with being able to meet those loan payments. Things you never could have thought of. Like my husband, Bob, dying last spring, then two months later my brush with cancer. Yep, I'd rather know that every board and log over my head at night is paid for in full.

The rest of the roof becomes a reality

Where the first half of our house roof went on so fast it seemed impossible, the second is dragging along. This is because on the south-facing side of the roof we are installing two very large dormers with large double-hung windows. Not only does this let in more sunlight and wonderful breezes through the opened window, but it adds a whole lot of extra useable floor space. As our roof is a 10 pitch, it slopes steeply from ridge to eaves. This gives us a lot of useable bedroom space upstairs and lets the heavy snow slide quickly off of the house. But with the addition of dormers, we can actually walk right to the eaves and look out a window without bonking our heads on the log rafter and roof boards.

To build the dormer (again, I could only afford the dormer in my bedroom along with the insulation and shingles up to the beginning of the dormer on my son, David's, dormer), the first thing that had to be done was to remove "old ugly," the well-worn silver tarp covering the roof. On the south side the tarp took a harder hit because of the sunlight. It was much more brittle and worn; it cannot be reused to cover hay as our tarp from the north side was. Because it would take several days to cut the dormer in, build it, and make it weather tight, David and Tom did not take it entirely off. Instead, it was thrown back and used as a tent each night, just in case it would rain. Ha, ha! We have had a severe drought all summer, so I thought we should leave the roof open and *make* it rain.

Once the roof was exposed, standing on his scaffold, Tom used his circular saw to cut the roof boards over the log rafter on either side of the new dormer opening. As we will be reusing the expensive tongue and groove 2x6s, Tom was very careful not to damage them in removal. Starting at the eaves, he pried them off of the center log rafter, which was going to be removed. As he took boards off, David pulled the nails and handed them to me to stack down in the basement. All of a sudden, we had a great open-air view of the small beaver pond and the woods. (Was that a rain cloud over to the west?)

The moment of truth came a few minutes later when Tom clamped the old jig left over from the building of the house over the rafter and leveled it up to use as a guide in making an absolutely plumb cut in the wall end of the log rafter. Then, firing up his chainsaw, he bravely cut through the rafter. Would the house fall down? Nah, not a creak. It was still held in place by the top roof boards and the lag screws into the opposing log rafter.

Using a Sawzall, he then cut through those log screws and the nails that held it to the boards—very gently—while David and I held the rafter from falling. It creaked as it came loose, but the wall end was against the wall and the top end was still on the ridge pole.

Getting on a ladder, Tom got his shoulder under the top end and David worked the bottom end, and they slowly wiggled it out of place and eased it to the floor. Hooray, it didn't drop through the floor into the kitchen!

Mom hadn't been upstairs in months, so David and I pulled/pushed her wheelchair up the stairs so she could see what all the commotion was about. She ooohed and ahhed and immensely enjoyed the view from the

The dormer wall going up.
That baby's 10 feet high and weighs 800 pounds!

huge hole. (Since that time, David went down with the chainsaw and removed a few trees so we have a much better view of the beaver pond from that window and the kitchen window. He would grab a tree and wiggle it. Standing in my bedroom window, I would shout "That one!" or "No, the one farther west!"

Okay, here we were, with a huge hole in the house. And David had to go help the neighbor hay. He'd been working for him all summer, and as the saying goes, he had to "make hay while the sun shines." So, off went David. Tom said confidently that he and I could frame the dormer wall and set it up. "It'll only weigh about 800 pounds." So what that if it fell on through the hole, it'd end up down 20 feet? But Tom is a confident person.

Taking careful measurements, he framed the dormer wall on the floor of my bedroom, with the bed squashed firmly against the north wall. The only problem was that the overhang of two feet on each side meant that the wall would be about four feet wider than the hole we would need to tip it out of. I shut up, helped, and figured that if it fell out and we didn't get killed, I guessed we could build another one.

He got it framed and sheeted, leaving an opening in the top for the log rafter that would be cut to make a functioning ridge pole (also attractive) for the dormer rafters. When sheeted with OSB, that puppy was heavy. The moment of truth arrived, and we grabbed a couple of four-foot 2x4s and started working it up. As it went up, Tom heaved first one overhang corner out, crawling out the window hole to drag it into place. In the meantime, I held the wall and made sure that the 2x4s were secure, bracing it fairly well in place. It reminded me of a huge rat trap, and I was the rat.

Once the first corner was outside, we heaved and heaved to twist the second overhang out so the wall would end up upright. First, we got it too high and the sill plate hung up on the butt of the rafter he had cut. Then we got it pried loose from there, and it didn't want to drop down into place. But finally, with the help of a crowbar, it slipped snugly into place and didn't fall out the opening.

A few spikes later, we stopped for a break and a couple of cold Mountain Dews.

Then, with a double header of 2x8 over the window and extra vertical framing on each side of the window opening, Tom framed the open space over the window, leaving a hole for the ridge pole to fit into. It would rest on top of the house's ridge pole and be supported by the framing on the wall side.

So here we are; still no David, and it's time to hoist the new ridge pole. But it went pretty good, actually. Tom slid the wall end through the wall opening while I held the other end, balanced on the ladder. That end couldn't fall down, anyway! Then we swapped positions, and I held the log while he wiggled and dragged it into place on top of the ridge pole. It fit, and it looked great. A few very large spikes and it was captured for eternity.

He finished framing the dormer in the second day. It would have taken me a week, with all of the compound cuts involved. (Gee, those sure look like rain clouds over west.) That evening, David was back home. (They saw those clouds, too.) He helped Tom batten down the hatches, dragging the tattered, worn old silver tarp up and over the new dormer. It was framed, but not sheeted. Definitely not watertight.

But we were lucky. We desperately wanted rain, but I didn't want a foot of water in the house, and that old tarp was not waterproof at this stage.

The next day, we sheeted the roof of the dormer and

Mom enjoys the view from the dormer-to-be.

started in on the main roof. Work went slowly at this point, as there were so many compound measurements and cuts for all the material, along with more flashing along the edges of the dormer where it met the main roof. Without adequate flashing underneath the shingles, the roof will eventually leak. Our old homestead ranch house in New Mexico had this problem. Someone had roofed over the old shake roof with corrugated sheet metal roofing and had not bothered to put in flashing in the valleys. Every time it rained, we discovered new leaks. We constantly fixed what we could, but were never happy with the underlying construction mistakes.

It took nearly two weeks to get that part of the roof finished, including the dormer. The dormer took about a week, then the next week went into finishing off the insulated roof. Tom also cut holes in the roof for our vent pipe for the drain on the kitchen sink and the tub that we'll put in the dormer of my bedroom. (A very nice *BHM* reader wrote and offered me his used, but in great shape, Metalbestos chimney for my wood kitchen range. Thank you so much!)

We didn't shingle down to the eaves this time because next spring I want to add a full porch on the south side of the house, 16' of which will be a year-round green room so I can grow food for the table and not have to pay $3.99 for a pound of fresh and very tasteless tomatoes or green peppers. This strip of the roof was covered with Typar and then Weather Watch ice shield and left until we build again next spring.

Right now, I'm regrouping financially until I can get enough to finish up the roof with the dormer in David's bedroom and the remaining insulation/shingles. It looks like construction will be starting soon.

The garden is attacked

About the time I was patting myself on the back for how great the garden looked, we started having trouble. Rows of beans were being chopped down. Corn came up missing. Terrorists? Well, in a way. They had four legs and soft brown eyes. Bambi and company decided my garden looked like a deer restaurant. I was in the process of fencing it.

My first crop of cukes and summer squash fill my market basket.

We had had deer in it last year, but they didn't bother it until late fall, after most everything had been harvested. Not so lucky this year, though.

I had bought 8' steel T posts, before they went up in price, along with a 100' roll of six-foot 2"x4" welded wire fencing. We had cleared a strip of brush (the garden is going to be enlarged this fall) and unrolled the wire. But David began working as soon as school was out, and with me being only 5' 2", I can't reach up to pound 8' posts from the ground. So it hadn't gotten done. I had figured on fencing one side at a time.

Well, the deer didn't come in from that side; they didn't want to wade over the down fence. It was propped up on small trees. So, they came in from the creek side instead. I carried steel posts down there and then went for the step ladder. My bum knee was much better, but climbing was not very fun. I stood up one post at a time, slid the driver on, and while clutching the ladder with my toes, I pounded posts. I did two at a crack, then went to sit down on the garden bench.

I did the corners first, then stretched out a piece of lightweight electric fence wire tightly to mark my line so the fence would end up straight. I got the posts in, but because of the roofing expense, I couldn't afford to buy 6' fence rolls. I had some 4' welded fencing left over from another project, so I used that. I figured it would help until I could afford better. And maybe they'd stay out for awhile.

Yeah, right. They walked around it and again munched down my regrowing crops. And started in on my first green tomatoes, just like apples. So, I drove more posts on that side of the garden and put up more 4' fence. And I tried a few natural spray/sprinkle-on deterrents to try and buy time until I got the garden totally fenced. I used hot pepper spray, rotten egg-type sprays, and blood meal. They all worked. Until I watered. Then it was free lunch again. And at $12.99 a bottle and a 100'x75' garden, I was going broke doing something that wasn't working.

And, don't tell me I should have used predator urine. In Montana, we let our wolf-malamute hybrid run in the garden during the winter and early spring. The deer never minded his pee. I don't figure they'd care about bottled coyote pee, either. By the way, I've tried "marking" the edges of my gardens with my own urine, as I've read some folks have had success with that. All I got was briar scratches all over my hind end. And all I could think of was, "Sure, now is when the neighbors will come calling!"

To make a long story short, I ended up fencing the entire garden, first with 4' wire, which was easy for a single person applying the fence. Then, I added another 3' of wire on top of that, to raise the height. Yes, the deer did jump over the 4' fence, but it took them just long enough for me to come up with enough money to buy more fence.

As soon as I totally got it fenced better than 6' high, I stopped having midnight callers in the garden. Mid-day, too. One day before I was done, I went down to water and a

The first canning corn of the year.
Three ears filled a pint jar.

155

big fat doe was standing in my sweet corn. I asked her politely what she was doing in my garden and I'll swear she said, "Your garden? I thought it was my garden!"

David hauls railroad ties with our old moving dolly. (Framed flower beds in background.)

I yelled, and she skipped off. With sweet corn breath blowing back on me.

The deer quit, then the ground squirrels started. And the little buggers fit nicely through the 2" spaces in the fence. The marauders I'm talking about are Richardson's Ground Squirrels. They are grayish, long-bodied gophers with a long hairy tail. They look kind of like a mongoose. And they have cheek pockets like a chipmunk. Boy, can they stuff a lot of your garden in those cheeks, too.

Now I love all animals, but I declared war on the ground squirrels. First I tried leaving out grain to see if I could bargain with them. I'd give them grain, if they'd leave my melons alone. I did, and they ate holes in every watermelon that began ripening. Enough is enough. I got out the .22. I figured if I shot a couple of them, the rest would become frightened and go back to the brush. Ha.

I ended up shooting one or two a day, but after awhile, there was only an occasional ground squirrel and they were content to eat the grain I left out to bargain with the chipmunks, who also enjoy my garden. They like to eat my tomatoes.

Every tomato that began ripening was eaten into. But that was easy to deal with; I just picked all the lower tomatoes just before they were ripe. They ripen fine in the house. I leave a few runty ones for the chipmunks, along with the grain, and we are all happy. I can't bring myself to shoot chipmunks; they're just too cute, and they were Bob's favorite critter.

Canning, canning, and more canning

This spring, I started all of my cucumbers, melons, and squash in our temporary greenhouse, and I was not disappointed with the results. To protect my precious Hopi Pale Grey squash seedlings, I covered them with a 4'x4' mini-hoop house made of leftover 2x4s and ¾" PVC pipe. I had deer eat my squash and pumpkin vines before, and I was not going to have that happen with the Hopis.

In short climates, it is just about necessary to start these long-season vining crops indoors to get a substantial crop. So, I had planted little vines 6" tall in their spaces in the garden. And they took off like wildfire. Luckily, with our water line being reworked when it was dug in last fall, our little submersible pump now puts out about 14 gallons per minute, compared to the tiny 3 gallons last year. So we were easily able to run lots of water on the garden during our long, very dry summer. And those vine crops especially liked it.

Because our garden is still small for my needs, I planted my carrots and bush beans in double rows, eight inches apart. That worked wonderfully and I'll never plant single rows again. Likewise, I pounded in steel posts on either end of my cucumber row and tied rolled stock fence from the dump on them. I had planned to trellis the cukes, so had ordered Japanese Climbing Cukes and Summer Dance, both straight, very long cucumbers that climb. Now climbing cucumbers do climb, but as they grow you have to gently pick up the growing end and poke it through the fence, higher and higher. The vines have strong tendrils that hold it in place very quickly and the vines will then support huge crops of footlong cukes.

And, it wasn't too many weeks into summer when I got my first "small" picking from those vines. I pick into a Vietnamese market basket because it holds lots, and I can balance it on my head to make carrying heavy loads easy. The bottom is soft on the head and when I get to the yard, I can rinse the vegetables at the hose. The excess water drains out due to the relatively loose weave.

My basket was nearly full of nice long cukes, so I set about making our favorite Bread and Butter pickles. These are sweet, crisp, and fast and easy to can. Because of our move from Montana in the dead of winter, my pickles had all gotten frozen and gone soft, so I lost them all. Having a big shelf full of pickles of all different sorts was looking so good.

Here's how I do my quick Bread and Butters, in case you want to try them:

Bread and Butter pickles

14 long slim cucumbers (or more short slim ones)
3 medium large onions
1 green bell pepper
1 red bell pepper
5 cups sugar
5 cups vinegar
1 Tbsp. mixed pickling spice with NO hot dried pepper
1 Tbsp. whole cloves
1½ tsp. turmeric
1 tsp. celery seed

Slice washed cucumbers, discarding stem and blossom end, then slice remaining vegetables and cut into bite-sized pieces. Mix well and put into large pan (I use a turkey roaster). Sprinkle with ½ cup pickling salt and pour ice-cold water on to cover pickles. Let stand overnight.

In the morning, drain well. In large pot, mix spices, sugar, and vinegar. I do not use a spice bag because I like the extra spiciness of leaving the whole spices in the pickles that I can. Bring mixture to a boil. Then pour over vegetables and bring to a boil. JUST bring it to a boil. If you boil the pickles, they will get soft.

Pack hot into pint jars, removing any air bubbles. Pour liquid over them to within ½ inch of the top of the jar. Don't overpack the pickles. Process for just 5 minutes in a boiling water bath. Have the water bath boiling when you put the pickle jars in it so the processing will go quickly. You don't want limp pickles.

That's it. When they are cool, check the seals, remove the rings, wash off the jars if they are sticky, and store in a cool, dark place. If you store in the light, they will lose their green color and become softer.

We love these pickles at most all meals. That's why they are called Bread and Butter pickles, because you eat them at meals like bread and butter. When I was a kid, I wouldn't eat them. I thought Mom had made them using bread and butter. In pickles? No way would I touch them.

But, then, our adopted son from India thought Americans made hot dogs from ground-up dogs. And he asked me while he was munching happily on his second hot dog, too.

Along with the Bread and Butter pickles, I made a few batches of quick dills, as the crop got heavier and heavier. I don't have time for brining them in a crock. And my quick dills taste just about as good, without all the days of skimming scum. Here's that recipe, too. Like the Bread and Butter pickles, they're very easy, fast, and tasty, too.

Quick dill pickles

18 lbs. small pickling cucumbers or the same longer ones to slice
9 cups water
6 cups vinegar
½ cup salt
½ cup sugar
2 Tbsp. mixed pickling spices
$1/_3$ cup mustard seed
7 cloves garlic (optional)
7 small dried pods of hot red pepper
fresh dill heads

Wash cucumbers well, removing blossom end if necessary. You may slice, halve, or quarter the cukes if they are larger. Put in large pan (I use the turkey roaster) and sprinkle with salt; cover with ice cold water. Let stand overnight. Drain and rinse cucumbers.

In a large pot, combine vinegar, water, salt, sugar, and the mixed spices tied in a spice bag, or not, as you prefer. Heat to boiling. Keep hot.

Place a head of dill in the bottom of each jar, then pack drained cukes in jar to nearly ½ inch of top. Place another head of dill on the top and also ½ clove of garlic (or more) and half a pod of hot red pepper (optional). Pour boiling pickling liquid over pickles. Put lid on jar and screw band tight. Process 20 minutes in boiling water bath (10 minutes if you have used slices). Makes 7 quarts or 14 pints, approximately.

Along with the cukes, soon the green beans and corn were starting to produce. I had only room for a small patch of sweet corn (I planted an early Kandy Kwik this year) and then the deer had eaten the rows down to stumps at least three times. So, of course, I had little hope to even get a couple of meals from it, let alone enough to can. But with the water and a good side-dressing of manure, that corn rebounded with energy. Finally, I saw ears with the tassels beginning to brown on the ends—a sure sign of maturity.

I squeezed an ear and found it nice and firmly plump. Then, carefully, I peeled a husk back and peeked in at the corn. Nice, shiny, fat yellow kernels peeped back at me. I picked enough for a meal for us, then looked up and down the rows.

Maybe, just maybe, I could can a small batch tomorrow? Would there be enough? I started picking in the morning and picked and picked. Soon, my market basket was full to overflowing, and I had picked only two rows.

Carrying it up to the round plastic table we have in the yard for outside food-processing chores, I began to husk corn. Behind me, I heard the fence creaking as all eight of our goats stood up, hungrily watching me. They knew I would give them the leftovers.

That table works so well for all kinds of work. Just the week before, our good friends, Jeri and Jim Bonnette, came over and helped us butcher five of our huge meat chickens. We used the table for plucking and dressing the birds, and it was so easy to use a garbage can for the waste, hose the table clean between birds, and be able to stand out in the open, not worrying about making a mess.

Likewise, when I pull carrots, I stop at the table, rinse them with the hose, then cut off the tops and root ends, giving them to the goats before I even take them into

"Bright Lights" variety of Swiss chard lights up our garden.

the house. Less mess in the house, and the goats sure like the extra treats.

I have one of those round, saw blade-type corn cutters I use for large batches of corn. It cuts real well, but I always end up cutting my left hand, as I hold the corn with that hand on the board and twist the cutter down over the cob with the other. I'm too frugal, I guess; I always cut down too far sooner or later and get myself. So on those little batches, I cut the corn off by standing it on end and using a sharp knife.

I pack the raw corn into pint jars to within an inch of the top, add a teaspoon of salt, and pour boiling water over the corn to within an inch of the top of the jar. It's that easy. Pints of corn are processed in the pressure canner for 55 minutes and quarts for 85 minutes at 10 pounds pressure (unless you live above 1,000 feet and must adjust your pressure accordingly; check your canning manual for directions).

Our family was getting so sick of "store" corn. It's always too mature, too tough, and has no taste. We had been living out of the pantry for three years, and my sweet corn had gotten down to two quarts and two pints, even with me hoarding it. Once you taste home-canned, home-grown sweet corn, you're spoiled for life. I have to laugh when folks ask me, "Why don't you just buy cans of corn at the store and not go through all that work?" Some people just don't know any better, I guess.

It's like telling me I should eat chuck roast instead of prime T-bone steak. No, thank you.

The yard gets a facelift

After more than two years of living on a raw gravel ridge, I was just itching to make our front yard a yard, not a parking lot. It is solid gravel, with tons of large stones; impossible to pick rocks to make a nice yard or flower beds.

Our friends, Jeri and Jim, asked David to come over and help them haul railroad ties out to their new garden. They garden exclusively in raised beds made of truck tires and railroad ties, and they needed more garden. So David went over and helped make beds. They are 24' long and about 4' wide.

Then, they ordered a big dump truck full of screened black dirt to fill them. I watched as the beds progressed when I came to pick up David and bring him to work. And the wheels began clicking in my head. Jim had gotten a big truck load of the ties for a "great deal" and had often offered me all the ties I wanted. So far I had waited, not knowing just what I wanted to do with them.

Last fall, another friend, Joe, came over to see if I would like some black dirt that the county had dug out of a ditch near his place. He told them to dump all they had "over by his garage" so he and his wife could have a little garden. He was away, and they dumped and dumped and dumped; all day long with several trucks. When they came home, there was a mountain range of black dirt out there and he couldn't get in his garage.

Joe knew we had a tractor with a loader on it, and he had an old, beater dump truck. So David went over and they hauled four big loads of black dirt over to our front lawn-to-be. Then his truck broke down and winter closed in with an ice storm. He could get in his garage, but didn't have much room.

In the spring, he asked if we would still like more black dirt. He only wanted enough to work up for a garden and there was still tons there. So I called our friend, Dale Rinne, who I knew had a track hoe and a big dump truck. Dale had hauled many loads of rock and gravel on our mile-long drive and was always quick, cheerful, and very fair.

Three days later, Joe had a nice level garden spot, and we had five more loads of black dirt on our yard, spread out fairly well. Dale also dug out our walk-out basement approach and even made me a large hole that will be a fish pond one day. As he also sold screened black dirt, I bought 10 yards from him, and he dumped it right in the yard where it would be handy for our beds.

So, here we were with nice black dirt on our rocky yard, and the offer of free railroad ties. What could I do? We built raised beds for flowers and herbs along the sides of the yard to hold back the woods and brush and make a place for our flowers that had been lacking for all this time. (By the way, if you are planning to use railroad ties for your vegetable garden, be aware that used ties are creosoted, but after years the creosote is leached and weakened. Enough is left to smell and protect them from rotting, but not enough to cause gardeners much concern. I have used them for years for raised beds and foundations for chicken houses and goat sheds.)

I dragged a heavy oak pallet over the area we would be making into the yard with our riding lawn mower/garden tractor, then we began laying out our beds. As an experienced bed-maker, David placed the ties, using our faithful moving dolly to haul them. Our beds along the north are 16' long and 4' wide. We cut ties in half to make the short ends, then spiked them together using 10" pole barn nails.

We left an 8' open space between beds in the event the propane tank needed replacing in the future. The gas man wouldn't like to back over a railroad-tie raised bed with his tank trailer. In this space, we just mounded a gentle hill of dirt without the ties.

On the end of the second north bed, I made an 8'x8' square with a 4'x4' square laid on top of the black dirt that filled the lower square. I had been envying my son, Bill, and his wife, Kelly's, circular strawberry tier garden, but I couldn't afford the cost. So we made our own version, and I love it. Two years ago, I had planted Fort Laramie strawberries down on a flat area below where our house now sits. But the deer had kept them trimmed, and they had only a few berries because I didn't water or care for them very well.

So I took a bucket down there and dug up 24 plants. They were nice and healthy, despite the deer munching, but they like it so much more in a well-watered raised bed. I carefully picked all grass out of the roots so I didn't plant grass (the #1 enemy of a strawberry patch) in my new bed, along with the strawberry plants. I dug down deep enough so the long, rank roots would comfortably fit with the crown just at soil level. (If you plant the crown too deeply, the plant will not do well and if you plant it so the roots show at all, the plant will die.)

Then, I watered the bed well, stood back, and smiled.

In the other beds, I've planted iris, fancy daylilies, sage, chives, and peonies. Mom is all excited about the new beds and has ordered fall bulbs, more lilies, peonies, and other perennials, so our garden will soon be full. I've always had lots of flowers. Some folks say it's a waste to plant things you can't eat. I believe that they're wrong. Where food satisfies your body, flowers feed your soul. ❧

Chapter Thirteen

When I look back on the last year, I am amazed at how far we've come! I recently ran across some pictures of the place two years ago, and where I'm sitting now there was nothing but a hole in the ground with a block and concrete basement. It has not taken huge sums of money or too much backbreaking work, just the focus to keep moving forward, no matter how tiny the steps seem at times. Those little steps add up to huge accomplishments, and it was all done without going into debt.

Staining the gable end

My son, Bill, said if he'd had it to do over, he would have put his log siding on his gable ends up without staining it right away. Since the logs were seasoned and the siding was not, the stain he used didn't match, making the siding an orangish color. I thought I'd better not make the same mistake, but soon I realized, as Tom nailed the siding up over insulation board, that his huge twenty-plus foot scaffolding would go home with him once he was finished. If I waited to stain that new siding until it had seasoned, then I'd be doing it from a twenty foot extension ladder and I'm scared of heights. So while Tom finished trimming the siding and windows, I grabbed a brush and gallon of stain and crawled out my bedroom window onto the scaffold planks.

I tried not to think about how far down it was, instead concentrating on nice even brush strokes. I'm glad I did it. The color doesn't match exactly, but it's not bad—as the wood weathers, the colors will more closely match. And the log siding is well protected from the elements,

165

being on the west side where our worst weather comes from.

Raising meat chickens

In spring, we got a great deal on 50 Cornish Rock broilers to raise for meat. I didn't want 50 myself, so we shared the purchase. Our friends, the Fishers, wanted some for their son's 4-H project, and a friend of theirs only wanted a dozen to butcher. The Fishers have a box stall in their barn to start the chicks in, so I bought the feed and went to get the 69 cent birds, and she raised them until they feathered out and the weather warmed up. It worked out well for all of us.

These broilers are meat machines and would gladly do nothing but eat and drink 24 hours a day. But because they gain weight so rapidly if they have free choice feed, when they get a few weeks old they have trouble with their legs. They go lame and finally die. To prevent leg trouble, we raised the older chicks separately from our other poultry. We kept food and water in front of them all day, but let the feed run out in the late afternoon. In the morning, they received feed for the day again. Several poultry houses recommended this tactic, and it worked well for us.

By the age of eight weeks, we could certainly have begun butchering them, but the temperatures were in the 80s and we had nowhere to chill

the meat, so we waited. By the time those birds were twelve weeks old and the weather had cooled, they were huge. I'm an old softie and cannot kill a chicken or anything else I've raised. Yes, I know, I go deer, elk, moose, and bird hunting, but I

Jackie stains the very high west gable logs.

can't kill one of my own chickens. Luckily my friends, the Bonnettes, are tougher and volunteered to come over and help butcher.

I can only handle putting up three birds at a time with very limited refrigeration, so we did five birds and I happily gave them two for their time and help. I made a butchering block out of a three-foot-high piece of pine log. Then I drove in two spikes, two inches apart, sticking up three inches or so, in the shape of a V. This way you can place the chickens' heads in the V, then behead them with a very sharp machete. I hid in the coop and caught birds, and felt guilty about it every time.

The next morning I cut the chilled chickens into pieces and set them to simmer on the stove. I used plenty of water to make sure all the meat was covered, added salt, pepper, sage, celery seed, and a little basil. Two ten- pound chickens filled my largest stock pot. It took two pots to boil up all three chickens. Unbelievable.

I simmered them most of the morning, then when the meat would easily come off the bone, I took the pots off the heat to cool down. The day was cool, so it was a perfect day to use natural refrigeration out in our temporary greenhouse. There the temperature hovered at 33° F, just right to cool the stock and meat down.

When it was cool, there was a thick layer of yellow grease on top. I carefully scooped this off to discard, because not only is all that grease unhealthy for us, but also because canning any meat with fat in the broth will often cause the seals to fail.

Then came the work. I carefully cut and pulled the breast halves apart and cut them so they would fit into wide mouth quart jars. As you leave one inch of head space in jars of chicken, I made sure that the pieces were cut to fit so they didn't stick up above that.

I cut the rest of the chicken into pieces and dices, and packed into regular mouth pint jars. I use regular mouth jars whenever possible to save money on lids. I poured all the stock through a sieve to strain out pieces of skin, etc. and into a clean stock pot to reheat to boiling. I then filled all the jars to within an inch of the top with boiling broth, wiped the rim

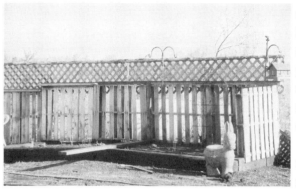

Salvaged pallets are screwed together with 2-inch deck screws and topped with lattice. Hopefully this new fence will help keep the deer out of the flower beds.

clean with a very hot, damp, clean cloth, and put a hot, previously simmered lid on, screwing the ring down firmly tight.

I usually can in my old, huge canner, so I stack quarts on the bottom and as many pints as will fit, then put a wire rack (made from a Dollar Store grill rack, and cut down to fit) on top of these, then stack the second layer with pints and half-pints.

When you can different size jars at the same time, you always use the longest processing time required, so in this case, the 90 minutes required of quarts, at 10 pounds pressure. (If you live at an altitude above 1,000 feet, you have to adjust your pressure to suit your altitude. Consult your canning manual for instructions.)

We repeated this whole process three times in the fall, and now I have only three of the smallest Cornish hens. I've decided to keep them along with my Araucana hens since they're starting to lay. I purposefully kept the smallest pullets because of the inherent leg problems that go with such heavy birds. Maybe I will be able to cross these with our old Araucana rooster and get some chicks that lay blue-green eggs and can up equally well.

More railroad ties

A while ago, David and I made two great flower and herb beds with old railroad ties that we were given by our friends Jim and Jeri. Well, the story gets better. Because their ties were stacked right where they want to park their vehicles this winter, Jim asked us if we could use a bunch more ties. Yeah! David borrowed a big tractor and rolled into the yard with a whole bunch of railroad ties stacked neatly on the hay forks behind!

In the days that followed, we drew up our game plan for more raised beds around the new yard. Some are now planted with lilies, daffodils, herbs, hollyhocks, Maximilian sunflowers, delphiniums, and wild tulips. Another is filled with sage and hardy thyme.

We'll use the rest of the ties to line the edge of the side yard next to the drop off into the old gravel pit. The old pit is now forested, so it doesn't look ugly, but the flower beds will add just the right break between the two levels.

Last fall, the deer were venturing into the new yard, sampling anything that was green. I really didn't want ugly wire fencing six feet tall around the house, so I started to gather pallets from town. It took all winter, but I got enough to build a 4 foot high, matched pallet fence with the solid side of the pallet toward the house, pickets upright. When we lived in Montana, I did this for the goat yard, screwing an eight-foot long 2x4 to the top and another 2x4 between the pallets to anchor them together. This eight-foot railing on top was anchored to two wood fence posts set in the ground two feet deep.

I'm putting this pallet fence behind the new flower beds to act as a backdrop for taller perennials and vines and on top of the pallets, I'm adding a 2x8-foot section of lattice, topped with a nice peeled pole to complete the rustic look and help keep Bambi at bay. I used 2-inch deck screws and my cordless drill, so it is strong and went together very fast. I think it looks nice, too—not at all like your "typical" ugly but serviceable pallet fence.

House update

We got our other dormer and roof finished just in time for cold weather. Thanks to Tom, we now have hot and cold running water in the kitchen, plus a wonderful salvaged antique clawfoot tub tucked into the

Salvaged clawfoot bathtub is all plumbed in. Artificial Christmas trees turn this into my "piney woods" secret bath dormer. I love it!

dormer of my bedroom, all plumbed in.

We also got our new-to-us wood kitchen range hooked up and operating. It sure saved lots of money on the propane bill last winter, and it made our little house feel like home.

All winter, we hauled loads of long, used power poles home from the reject pile at the power company. Now we're starting to build the porch on the south side of the house. Half of it will be a four-season garden room and the other half will be an enclosed porch.

Just in the last week, Tom, David, and I have been digging, hauling, and setting upright poles. These will hold up the floor and joist support beams.

Tom has an old two-man gas powered post hole auger with a 12 inch auger. It would probably dig a lot better if we didn't live on a gravel ridge. You start it and it kicks out softball-sized rocks and the digging jiggles out your gizzard. Then Tom has to shut it off and remove the rocks by hand, pull the auger out of the hole, use a crowbar to pry out more rocks and loosen the soil, then alternately use a manual post-hole digger and gallon-sized coffee can to dig the loose dirt out of the deepening hole.

Because our frost level is very deep, these holes have to be even deeper. Luckily both Tom and David are tall and have long arms. Even so, the holes get so deep that David has to hang down inside the hole to get the last dirt out.

The first post was very heavy and Tom and I set it ourselves, using our old Ford 8N tractor and bucket. We stuck a piece of 2x6 down in the hole to keep the butt of the pole from sliding past the hole, then we worked the pole toward the hole by chaining it to the tractor's bucket and alternately lifting the bucket and driving it forward. Then came the interesting part. The ground by the back of the greenhouse is sloped loose gravel, so traction is a problem. Tom would lift the pole, drive forward, then get stuck. Then we'd have to prop it up and re-chain it after he got the tractor free.

I felt like a fat rabbit in a deadfall trap with that huge pole looming over my head! Finally, we got it high and made the final chain-up to lift it into the hole. But during the lift, it slipped and put a bind on the chain and the rear wheel of the tractor lifted three feet off the ground! We couldn't loosen the chain, because everything was bound tight. We shoved a shorter piece of pole under the bucket and pried it a little to set the tractor back on the ground, then we wedged it there to hold things in place. We couldn't unhook the tight chain so Tom carefully pulled the pin on the hook, taking care that the chain didn't whip back at him.

It was time for "Plan B." I brought the truck around to face the trac-tor and chained the pole to the bumper to keep it from falling down the hill as we worked.

As he drove slowly forward, I inched backward to keep tension on the chain—not too much because we couldn't have the pole pulled off the

Sinking the salvaged telephone poles that will become the enclosed porch and garden room. We nearly tipped the tractor over with this one!

David hauls a big load of railroad ties for the new raised beds.

edge of the bucket—but then the tractor bucket bounced and the pole popped off. There I was looking right up at a 26 foot pole weighing 700 pounds, leaning right at me.

The butt was in the hole, maybe by two feet, but boy was it leaning my way. Luckily, Tom quickly got back under it and we soon had it dropped right into the hole. Luckily, the other poles went in much easier. Tom and David were able to work them in by hand since they were lighter poles.

Now we're ready to start framing the porch, and boy am I excited. It will be nice to have it all come together, especially since I've been using the temporary greenhouse to start our garden plants all this time.

The next garden

My garden starts in January. This is when I start inventorying my seeds to see what I will plant in the garden this year. A lot of my seeds are those I've saved from my own plants, especially tomatoes, beans, melons, and squash. Folks have given me some so I can try their family heirlooms. And like most folks, I also can't pass up the offerings in the seed catalogs that start to come in the mail in January.

Of course I order from some of the more well-known seed companies, but a few of my favorite companies are lesser known. You might like to check them out:

Seed Dreams
P.O. Box 106
Port Townsend, WA 98368
(They carry Hopi Pale Grey squash seeds, my very favorite, nearly extinct squash.)

Pinetree Garden Seeds
P.O. Box 300
New Gloucester, ME 04260-0300
www.superseeds.com

Seed Savers Exchange
3094 North Winn Road
Decorah, IA 52101
www.seedsavers.org

Baker Creek Heirloom Seeds
2278 Baker Creek Road
Mansfield, MO 65704
http://rareseeds.com

Because we have always lived in a cold climate, having tasty varieties that actually make a good crop is vital to me. For instance, tomatoes that require longer than 90 days to ripen just don't make it past my first glance.

Every year I make sure to plant my old standbys, but I also like to try new varieties—after all, I never know when I'll find a new favorite.

Some varieties that I come back to year after year are:

Tomatoes: Early Cascade, Polish Linguisa, Early Bush Beefsteak, Oregon Spring, and Stupice.

Peppers: Parks Early Thickset, Giant Marconi, Aconcagua, Roumanian Rainbow, Fat 'N' Sassy, and Early Jalapeño.

Some of my favorite squash at harvest. From top, Flying Saucer, Hopi Pale Grey, American Tonda Pumpkin, and Golden Marble Pattypan

Beans: Beans are a staple, plus they are so fun and easy to grow, so I grow plenty! After all, I can lots of them, and the dry beans keep for years. My favorites include Cherokee Trail of Tears, Provider, Dragon Tongue, Roma, Golondrina (or Frijol Chivita), and Paiute Pinto. This year I'm also trying a dozen other varieties.

Corn: My usual corn patch for cornmeal is Painted Mountain, which makes a dry corn in 90 days. I also grow a hybrid sweet corn because it is so early, usually Kandy King. I also maintain a little patch of True Gold, which is open-pollinated, so I can save seed, but it's pretty late and doesn't always ripen fully here in our cool climate. I grow Tom Thumb and alternately Robust yellow hybrid popcorn.

Corn requires a mile separation between varieties or a varying pollination time, so I seldom grow more than three varieties a year to keep them from cross-pollinating. The rest of my favorites I have to rotate every few years, but they include Native American corns such as Hopi Chinmark, Santo Domingo Blue, Cherokee White Flower, and Cocopah sweet corn.

Carrots: I like Tendersweet and Kuroda carrots as they're not only tasty, but very large and can up quickly. As they get large, the thinnings make great salad and stir fry ingredients.

Melons: Watermelons in northern Minnesota? You bet! My favorite watermelons are Blacktail Mountain, OrangeGlo, Moon and Stars, and San Juan.

Likewise, we grow several varieties of muskmelon. My old standbys are Navajo Yellow, Minnesota Midget, Fastbreak, Alaska, and Noir De Carmes.

Fancies: As you can see, I not only like productive, flavorful vegetables, but pretty ones, too! This is why I grow Bright Lights Swiss chard, Scarlet Runner beans, and trellised cucumbers of the long-straight Asian types, such as Summer Dance, Tasty Green Hybrid, and Japanese Climbing, as well as the pickling varieties Homemade Pickles and Chicago Pickling for tiny sweet pickles and dills. Those huge, slender Asian cukes make tons and tons of bread and butter pickles and sliced dills, but they are too slender for regular dills and sweet gherkins.

Squash: Of course, I always grow my very rare Hopi Pale Grey squash, along with several different species of squash. (To keep pure seed, you must take care that different varieties of the same species don't cross. This may be done with spacing or the timing of different flowering if you have enough growing season. I don't, so I only grow one Cucurbita maxima and that's Hopi Pale Grey. But I do grow Goldbar and Flying Saucers summer squash which are C. pepo, Ponca Butternut, Magdalena Big Cheese (a C. moschata), and others in rotation.

Potatoes: My potatoes don't vary too much. I always grow Yukon Gold as they not only look gorgeous but produce abundantly and taste great. Then I grow Red Norland and Anoka for their taste and productivity, plus Russian Fingerling or Ozette Fingerling for their waxy, nutty flavor.

Greens: Then there are beds of mixed salad greens, lettuces of all different colors and shapes, Goliath broccoli, herbs of a wide variety, from sage to epazote. And we can't forget spinach, usually Bloomsdale Long Standing and Tyee for their taste and productivity.

Root crops: Our favorites are American Purple Top rutabagas, White Globe turnips, and Harris Model parsnips. We grow lots of these, especially now that we have a great root cellar to keep them in.

Our little homestead may be a little shaggy in some areas, but we're up and running. The orchard looks like slash piles and wild raspberry bushes, but the trees survived winter and are growing. The chicken coop/goat barn still has tarps on one gable, but the critters are dry and warm. And we are now living in a relatively finished small but very cozy log home. All built owing no one except for the goodness of God and our faithful family and friends. It's a good feeling, indeed. 🌿

Chapter Fourteen

When I look back over the last year, I can scarcely believe so much has happened here on our homestead. It's amazing at what can be crunched together into a few months. And now it's late fall and again we're getting ready for winter. But let me tell you what we've been doing (along with why we didn't get more done).

Bill and the crawler

When the temperatures warmed up in May, I was dying to get the garden planted. But my oldest son, Bill, said he'd come up again with his crawler and do some enlarging and grading for me. I didn't want to plant, then have things in his way, so I waited. Bill's a busy guy with work, helping neighbors, and building on his own homestead. But one day he came up the trail with his Case crawler chained down to his flatbed trailer. I was really tickled because we have kind of rough land, having been partially logged about fifteen years ago. I needed the orchard cleaned of brush, log piles, ruts, and rocks; the garden enlarged; and the trail down to the horse pasture widened. Our little 9N Ford tractor just wasn't up to that much pushing.

Bill set right to work in the garden. He shoved old dozer piles down the hill, flattening them out so they wouldn't be such an eyesore, pushed little popple trees over, leveled and graded the garden area, and dug up a few big old stumps that were a real problem. When he got done, all but a 10-foot area next to the fence was clean, level, and smooth. My garden had suddenly doubled in size, and we sure needed it. Now it's about 60 feet by 100 feet. When we started here, I had a spot only 25 feet by 10 feet after clearing it all by hand.

Next Bill started in on the orchard, which was basically some young fruit trees planted amongst wild raspberries, rocks, logs, and piles a dozer had left years ago. Ugly? Oh yeah! Bill carefully shoved debris around my little fruit trees, taking great care not to get too close to them. I had marked some good wild cherry and chokecherry trees (and my orchard trees!) with flagging tape, as well as a few pretty birch trees I wanted to save along the edges. When Bill got done, the orchard was quite flat and clean.

I want to fence it with 6-foot-tall 2 by 4-inch welded wire to keep the deer out. Right now most of the trees are individually fenced and have their trunks protected with screen to keep voles, rabbits, and field mice from girdling them. But the deer can still reach over and nibble a bit. I also want to have the chickens in the orchard, running free inside the fence to keep down the grass and weeds, and also to keep them out of my flower beds!

Right now, our little orchard is about 60 feet wide by about 150 feet long. We have Haralson, Haralred, Honeygold, Honeycrisp, Fireside, and Yellow Transparent apples growing in there. We'll add other fruits next year. Down in the garden, we have planted a Pipestone plum, some Manchurian apricots, and smaller bush and bramble fruits so far.

While Bill was here, he also rooted up a lot of stumps in our horse pasture, widened the trail down there, and opened up a four wheeler trail around the hill.

Bill also dug a small test hole at a spring site below the house. We wanted to see how long it stayed full. It was full except for three weeks during the drought that lasted all summer. Now if it was deeper and developed…

The garden

As soon as Bill left, David and I quickly set about pounding the steel T posts on the garden fence line and stretching the 6-foot welded wire back up tight. I was not going to have deer in my garden again this year—and I didn't.

I tilled up most of the garden and got it planted. It was getting late and you don't plant late in northern Minnesota if you can help it. Even my tomatoes and peppers, in their Wallo' Waters, went in a month later than they should have. Even so, it was worth it to get the garden made so much bigger. Since we were late, we planted and planted and planted. I don't think I've ever worked so frantically to get a garden in.

Jim Bonnette shows some of our "leftover" green beans.

Because we were also starting on the new greenhouse/porch, I hadn't been able to start my squash and melons inside as I usually do. I just hoped we'd get lucky. (We did.)

After we got the main part of the garden planted, I started hand clearing the last ten feet of garden that Bill couldn't get to because of the fence. David brought the tractor down and we pulled about a dozen 10-foot-tall popple trees out by the roots. (By the way, for you non-Minnesotans, "popple" is the northern nickname for poplar trees, or in the west, aspen.) I've found that it's better to pull smaller trees, rather than cut them off. Not only do you eliminate stumps and root masses, but also the many sprouts that tend to come up from the roots.

I took a large pair of hand clippers and cut off all the brush I could, as low as I could. Then I tossed all the rocks, logs, and branches over the fence as I came to them. After the area was relatively clear, I tilled it a few times. It was kind of rough, but it did get worked up. Then I would do another strip about 2 feet wide or so until I got to the fence. When it was all worked up nicely, I looked back on it and thought about it. Here was this nicely worked 10-foot strip, 100 feet long. Would anything grow on it, or would it just grow up to brush again?

I couldn't stand it. I'd already planted plenty of beans, potatoes, melons, and squash, but I got out the seed again and went to town. I also planted rutabagas and parsnips.

The only problem was that when harvest came, I canned green beans every other day until I had a whole two-foot deep shelf full. So I called my friends Jim and Jeri (whose goats had broken into their green beans) and invited them to come pick green beans. As it ended up, we both had way plenty!

A new chipper

Our big spring purchase this year was a chipper. We'd been talking about one for years. Here we have all these trees to get rid of, brush, branches, debris, and we need lots of mulch. It only made sense. So when one went on sale, I took our saved money to town and came home with "Big Red." David couldn't wait to fire it up. I was a little disappointed because I thought once you shoved a branch in that it would grab it and pull it on through. It doesn't. I guess they changed them for safety reasons. On the plus side, all we had left after we chipped those trees was a pile of nice wood chips that served to mulch the asparagus and raspberries nicely.

We are enjoying it. I would have liked to get a big DR model chipper, but our little savings just wasn't big enough. Big Red is working fine, albeit a little slow. David ran the spent corn stalks and tomato vines through it and it made very fine material that worked in on the first pass. Of course, being a boy, he just had to toss in a few squash,

Tom and David notch in the support beam on the new porch this spring.

frozen tomatoes, and broccoli plants! "Wow Mom! Look at that!"

David vs flesh-eating bacteria

The garden was growing nicely, the new greenhouse/porch was under way, and David was haying for our neighbor again this year. Bill had invited David down to go camping with him and his wife, Kelly, for the Fourth of July. But the morning of the 3rd, when he was getting up to leave, he said he must have snored because he had a little sore throat. And his first knuckle on his left hand was kind of sore. He must have thrashed around in his sleep and banged it.

By 10 pm, Bill called to say David was sick. He was cold, droopy, and his hand was swelling. I agreed that David better head for the emergency room. So they put out the campfire and drove to the hospital in Cloquet.

At the hospital, the doctor thought David had poked something into his knuckle, starting an infection in his hand, so they kept him and started IV antibiotics. When I drove down the next morning, I expected him to be better. Instead the swelling was getting worse and he was in intense pain. The following morning the swelling was going up his arm, along with a red streak. Was I panicked? Oh yeah! I got a healthy flashback to when Bob had died, and I started to shake.

181

Luckily, David's doctor had called the infectious disease specialist in Duluth and she told them to get a CT scan of his hand and arm and get him up to St. Luke's Hospital for immediate surgery. She believed it was flesh-eating bacteria and that even with immediate surgery, she wasn't sure they'd be able to save his arm.

To make a long story shorter, David had the surgery, then another one a couple days later. Both were very successful. He came home a week later with a main line IV hooked to a little computerized pump that he wore around his waist in a belly pack. This was a part of his life for another three weeks to maintain heavy duty antibiotics to prevent any possible recurrence.

Tom spiking the rafters down

Of course David didn't wimp around; two weeks after his surgery, he was back on the tractor, haying...IV and all. Later, the doctors all said they'd never seen anyone heal up so well, so quickly.

I learned a lot about flesh-eating bacteria. It didn't come from a cut, nick, poke, or sliver. It came from the mild strep infection in his throat. The doctor said that one in a million type A strep infections breaks loose and goes through the bloodstream to lodge in an extremity—a foot, hand, or even head/brain, where it causes intense pain. The bacteria produces a toxin which eats the muscle covering, causing necrosis. And it moves very quickly. The doctor said that in another day, David would have lost his arm and in one more, he could have lost his life. I tell everyone I talk to about his experience in the hopes that should this ever happen to someone in their family that they would be better informed than I was. We were very lucky—blessed!

Football season started about three weeks after David had his 37 staples and 12 stitches removed, and had the IV line pulled out of his chest. He badly wanted to play this year, but figured he wasn't recovered enough to play. Within three weeks he was back at karate and had the doctor's go-ahead to play. He had an awesome season as both kicker and on defense. Needless to say, I'm a very proud mom!

The house

Our little log house is growing. After we got those huge used power poles in the ground early this spring, we set about getting the greenhouse/porch put together. Tom, our carpenter friend, is a very handy guy. Special pole floor joist supports cost $200 each and we were going to need several. So instead he took measurements, went to a steel salvage yard in Hibbing, and welded his own version. Basically, they're cup-shaped brackets that fit under the house end of the log and lag screw to the sill plate.

Each pole floor joist was lowered into the bracket and spiked to the sill plate. The other end was notched to fit over the long log ledger plate, which in turn was notched into each upright post and bolted securely into place. It was a lot of scribing, cutting, and work, but Tom made steady progress fitting the whole floor support system together. It was especially tricky working over the basement walk-out area. You can't stand there, let alone hoist a heavy pole into place. So Tom used a come-along to lower and support the pole while he notched it to fit. Ingenious—and a whole lot safer than a person teetering on a ladder.

When the joists were in place, the 2 by 6 tongue and groove flooring was cut and nailed down. In two days, we had a porch!

I'd learned a lesson from upstairs in the house: seal the floor right away! The upstairs floor got all marked up by us walking back and forth on it. It's still not finished! I picked out a nice reddish brown color that I thought would match the house logs well. The next day I got out the brushes and roller and had at it. Gasp! That new stain/sealer was this God-awful orange! I thoroughly restirred the stain. And I did another large chunk. Yep. Orange. By then it was too late to do anything but finish the floor—all 30 feet of my nice pine orange floor. The pail said you couldn't recover it if it was dry and to give it multiple coats while it was still damp, which I did. Boy what a job! And no matter what I did, there were streaks. Great. Orange with streaks. It looked like a five year old had stained my porch. It was not a happy day.

But in a couple of days, the color began to mellow out. The orange tamed down and finally died. It became that nice reddish brown I'd hoped for. And the streaks went away too. Where? Who cares? Whew!

The pole rafters were next. One end was tapered and supported on the house roof, over the log rafters of the roof. To support the other end, Tom built a box beam from 2x12s and a 2x8. This puppy was 38 feet long and when Tom said he, David, and I would just "lift it right up" to get it atop the upright posts, I thought he was nuts. Well, we did. Three guys on one end made the job doable. Tom had notched out the tops of the uprights, leaving a shoulder for the 2x12 to sit on. The 2x8 sat on top of the uprights. When the whole thing was up, it slid right into place with very little help.

The next day, the rafters started going up. They went quickly, too. They were the smaller poles we'd saved for the purpose, so they were easier to handle and notch to fit the box beam. Next we put in the rafters in between the pole rafters in the greenhouse area, which would be insulated. On top of that was a layer of insulation board and OSB of a thickness to match the tongue and groove fir 2x6s that made the roof of the rest of the porch. (And also the ceiling, as you look up from the porch.) Tom framed cutouts for the three skylights we planned to put in: one over the kitchen window, one over the living room window, and one in front of the doorway

The new porch—a relaxing place to cut beans or corn or just sit

into the living room from the porch. These not only let in a lot of light but one is able to be opened for ventilation in the greenhouse.

We went along pretty slowly for a while; those skylights were over $400 each! But one by one, I got them and Tom put them in. And finally we were ready to enclose the four-season greenhouse. We had some salvaged patio door window glass so we put in one of them in the center space in the greenhouse. In the spring we're going around the corner with the addition, so we put up three of the others as a temporary wall on the east end. It lets in the light and keeps out the cold. In the spring, we'll take them down and continue on, reusing them again.

Oh, by the way, you remember the old Filon (corrugated fiberglass) we had used on our greenhouse addition at the mobile home, then again last year on the temporary greenhouse on the house? Well we carefully saved it and it is now on the east side of the goat barn! And it lets in a whole lot of light, too. The junk OSB David and I had nailed down two years ago kept the snow out, but it leaked and was a real nasty looking fix. The new roof doesn't leak. I stopped up all the holes with a squirt of silicone sealer.

Now the greenhouse is all insulated with fiberglass on the inside, then sided with half log siding and 1"x5" pine tongue and groove paneling that we got on sale because of its off-sizing. It looks very nice, and it's warm too.

Right now we've got ripe tomatoes and peppers all over the place. The plants are just recovering because I moved them so many times. But they are mostly setting new, greener leaves and are perking up with a good dose of manure tea. They did get quite an infestation of aphids while they were stressed, requiring me to spray them twice with water soluble rotenone. They didn't need those tiny, juice-sucking bugs on the underside of their leaves. I was tipped off when I saw a ladybug on one of the plants—they just love aphids. I freed the ladybug outside before spraying the plants, since the rotenone would have killed my tiny helper.

Right now, I'm finishing staining the inside logs and wood of the greenhouse. When that's all done, I'll be planting some tubs of greens, carrots, and maybe even some broccoli. Broccoli was $2.89 a pound at the store yesterday. I can pack eight plants into a large plastic storage bin full of soil. That will give us lots and lots of broccoli during the winter.

A lot of people don't grow broccoli because they figure they'll only get one head per plant. Not so. Once the main head has been cut, the plants produce tons of side shoots, some nearly as big as the central head. And this will go on until the plants freeze out in late fall. Ours are just now finished.

Our very own bulldozer

One day during the summer haying season (after the flesh-eating bacteria episode), David came home all enthused. He had been haying a field owned by a neighbor lady who lost her husband early this spring. She was selling a lot of the farm equipment and had two bulldozers to sell. David had fallen in love with a big yellow John Deere 1010 crawler. I think Gail was just humoring David when he said that I might buy it. After all, how many women buy a bulldozer? But I thought the asking price was low enough to make it a real deal and knew her late husband maintained his equipment well. So I went over that evening.

Not only could we really use a bulldozer on our new homestead (and this one cost less than most cheap used cars), but I figured that at 16, David could learn a lot driving and maintaining one. He had already had extensive experience on several large tractors that his boss, Mr. Yourczeck, owns, but also our own 9N Ford, and a little time with his brother Bill's Case crawler. A man who can operate heavy equipment can always find a well-paying job, despite the economy's upheavals. Call it a life skill.

I only had one more payment left on the Ford 250 plow truck, so I figured I could refinance that to buy the dozer; it's our only monthly bill. I didn't like to borrow again but knew the dozer wouldn't last long, once word got out. I called our handy friend Tom and asked him if he'd be willing to do repair/maintenance on it in exchange for using it on his homestead. He agreed. (Tom is good on mechanics, can weld, and is also a figure-it-out sort of young man.) So I went in to the bank that next morning with a picture David had taken of the dozer. The young lady who was the loan officer asked what she could do for me, and almost needed an assistant to get her chin up off the floor when I said I wanted to buy a bulldozer.

Well, we've had the dozer for better than three months now and I can tell you that it's been a great addition to our homestead. It cost $100 each way in gas for Bill to haul his crawler up to our place, so we didn't

David, learning to run our new bulldozer by grading the goat yard. Notice the old siding on the chicken coop.

use it often. (It's also a big imposition for me to ask him to bring it up because he is a very busy man...and will be even busier because he and Kelly are expecting in December!)

David started right in and quickly learned the ropes operating the dozer. He started off kind of gently by pushing some level spots next to our driveway to park the vehicles. Then he cleaned in front of the goat barn/chicken pen, moving right on to scrape out the donkey pen. Soon after, he cleared out some trails down in the horse pasture and dug out many old stumps. Now we can access our big woods to haul logs and firewood home. We couldn't get the tractor or pickup down there before.

We've had a few minor setbacks with the dozer. Like the time David was clearing brush around his best deer stand and threw a track. Now the track is really heavy. Think tank track! He knew that to take the pressure off the track tightener (which is tightened with grease pressure), he had to let grease out of the housing. He took off a cap screw and shoved in on the track. Yeah, grease came out and we got the track back on with heavy pry-bars. But when he went to tighten the track again with the grease gun, grease squirted out from under the tightener!

We finally found out from my good friend, Will, that we had squirted out a ball bearing with the first gob of grease. That ball bearing acts as a valve. I belatedly read the directions (doesn't that sound familiar?), finding out that you loosen the cap screw, which lets grease squirt out from underneath, but you don't take it off all the way. Oops!

Luckily, Nortrax in Duluth knew just what we needed and sent us a beautiful little shiny ball bearing which David dropped into the hole. And the track magically tightened! Dad used to say, "Too soon old, too late smart!" Oh so true.

Now David is clearing a spot next to the horse pasture for a nice training ring for me. As it's all sand, it will be perfect. It's nearly done now and all I've got to do is find someone who sells cedar fence posts. It would be nice to get the ring graded and the fence posts put in by freeze up. It's going to be close as it's already dipping into the teens at night.

There's quite a trick to learning how to clear land nicely with a bulldozer. If you just lower the blade and shove forward, you'll end up with huge, ugly piles of dirt/roots/tree parts. But if you work it back and forth a little as you clear, the trees will be separated from the dirt, leaving most of the dirt and letting the trees be piled for later cutting and/or burning. We cut up everything we can use for firewood, chip what works, and pile the rest (usually rotten stuff) for burning during the winter. David is learning to run up on the pile of dirt, spreading it out nicely so as not to leave mounds of debris.

The first trips over an area to be cleared skins off the trees, brush, stumps, and topsoil (it contains roots and brush). If we are going to plant an area, the topsoil is carefully worked free of most debris and piled aside to push back on the area it came from. In the case of the training ring and our hay area, the topsoil is graded over debris nice and smooth. Then in the spring I'll seed it in with grass and clover. The deer will just love me! The spots where Bill shoved the orchard debris over the hill, are now nice flat, lush mini-pastures and have deer in them every day.

Canning update

Although our summer was one of severe heat and drought, the garden did amazingly well. Luckily, I was able to keep it well watered. Neighbors who could not because of failing wells lost much of their produce. I planted a big patch of Kandy Korn and another of a bicolor Kandy Korn sister. Because most of the corn was on a dry, unfertilized slope, it took the drought kind of hard. Some of the stalks were shorter than normal, and the ears were smaller. It sure showed me where I needed to spread some rotted manure this fall.

Luckily I planted a lot of corn. I had 14 rows 25-feet long, so I had a lot of corn to both eat regularly and can up. I would have had much more, but that's the breaks. It's also why I always can up all I can when

I have it. Who knows what next year might bring?

I love canning sweet corn. I just pick a big basket full, carry it up by the goat pen, and shuck it on my old handy-dandy white plastic table. The goats line up on their fence, knowing that they get all the shuck, silks, and any poor ears.

Then I carry the corn inside and get to sit out on my lovely (unfinished as of harvest) new porch and cut the corn off the cobs onto cookie sheets. I've got a corn cutter that you hold and shove down over the cob. They say in the advertising that you can hold the handles with each hand and just push it down easily to remove the kernels. Ha!

I end up working the handle back and forth, while pushing down hard, and holding the cob in place on a cookie sheet with the other hand. It does work well, but I always end up trying to get every little bit of corn off the cob and cutting my hand by the base of my thumb when the saw thing gets too close. "Mom! Don't bleed in the corn!"

Anyway, I pack the fresh corn into pint and half-pint jars to within an inch of the top, add a teaspoon of salt and pour boiling water on it to within an inch of the top of the jar. Corn is a long-processing food at 10 pounds pressure. You do pints and half pints for 55 minutes. But it's so good! A thousand times better than store canned corn. There's a huge difference, not only in taste, but in tenderness, too.

Usually, sweet corn produces two ears per stalk. This year, I got a few double ears, but the stalks seemed to quit growing very early, drying up. So as soon as I had picked the first corn, I went through the patch and cut all the stalks with no more ears on them or a very poor second ear. I give this to the goats, donkeys, and horses. They love it and it's good for them. It's good for the garden, too, as corn pests, such as corn ear worms, winter over in corn stalks to become a bad pest in following years. So corn stalks are one thing I remove from the garden.

As I told you, my green beans were super productive. My yellow beans were on the non-fertile end of the new garden and didn't do well, except for the Dragon Tongue. Holy mackerel, I like those beans!

They're huge, flat, long, and meaty. They do look a little weird, being purple and yellow striped, but it makes them easy to pick. The strange color disappears when you cook or can them. I canned Dragon Tongue beans as wax beans, then made mustard bean pickles out of a big batch of them. If you've never made these, you're missing a great taste treat. It's kind of like honey mustard pickles. After we use the bean pickles, I save the leftover sauce and we use it to dip chicken and pork in. It is very good and not real mustardy. Kind of sweet and sour.

Here's how you make them if you want to give it a try next year. While yellow beans make a prettier bean pickle, you can also use green beans—I sure did! (Did I mention I had **lots** of green beans this year? Ha! Ha!)

Mustard bean pickles:

8 quarts yellow wax beans
salt
6 cups sugar
1 cup flour
5 Tbsp. dry mustard
1 Tbsp. turmeric
6 cups vinegar

Cut beans in one-inch pieces and simmer in salted water until barely tender. Drain. Mix dry ingredients together in pan. Stir while adding vinegar. Bring to a boil. Add beans and again bring to a boil. Simmer five minutes. Pack hot into hot, sterilized jars, and water bath process for 10 minutes. Makes 8 pints.

Our cucumbers were also very productive. I planted Summer Dance and Japanese Climbing on a stock panel trellis. They did very good for my bread and butter pickles. The only thing I don't like about these very thin, long cukes is that they don't make pretty dill pickles. You have to cut them in half to get them to fit into a quart jar, and often into thirds, to fit into a pint. I had this trouble last year, so I planted Chicago

Part of our fall harvest in the new greenhouse. The floor color has mellowed to the reddish brown I had hoped for. Much better than the screaming orange.

Pickling cukes just for dills and whole sweet pickles. That worked much better, although they didn't like the heat much; they kind of went yellow and wilted. When the heat was over, they again greened up and started producing well again. My shelves are full of pickles of all sorts now.

I planted carrots between my rows of asparagus and black raspberries on kind of a gravelly hill, and they did not like it. Also, I didn't pull the grass out of the area, because that was right when David got sick. (Well, it's a good excuse, anyway.) So the carrots were slow. But my friend Jeri had more carrots than she needed, so I got to can a bunch of carrots anyway. At the very end of the season, I did get canning carrots out of my rows, but they weren't anything to brag about. I've already planned to move my carrots back down where I have nicer soil and it is more fertile.

I was extremely happy with my afterthought rutabagas and Packman broccoli in the new part of the garden. The rutabagas grew leaves near-ly waist high and had softball-sized roots in August. By late September, they were the size of soccer balls, and still tender and sweet, too. They stuck way up out of the ground. So far up that the @$*% deer ate the tops out of them after hopping the fence where a tree had taken it down in a wind storm.

I did salvage a lot of them by severe trimming. I was going to store them whole in the basement, in my new pantry. But damaged like that,

I diced them to can. I know the canning manuals say that rutabagas get discolored and strong tasting and aren't worth canning. But I haven't found that so. I do dump the canning water down the drain and heat them in fresh water. This seems to remove the cabbage smell and taste that is a little strong at times. I was hoping to save my pint jars for venison, but I bought a few boxes of jars, was given some, and went ahead and canned 'em up. Now I'm wondering how our rutabaga flavored venison will taste.

Yard update

This spring, our new front yard was nothing but black dirt with our new railroad tie raised beds full of perennials and bulbs hoping for new life. Well they got it! We got lots of spring rain and the grass sprouted beautifully, quickly turning into a real lawn. Our bare, cold winter killed a lot of the bulbs and perennials, but we still had a gorgeous flower show all summer. I did cheat and plant a bunch of annuals where there were bare spots. The color was sure worth it!

Our raised beds are turning out wonderful. I've got herbs at the head of the first bed and they love it. The chives need to be divided already and the oregano is climbing over the ties. But our two newest beds got black dirt that also had a lot of grass seed in it and boy what a job that is to keep out. I've still got a piece of daylily bed that needs weeding. With grass, there's nothing to do but pull it up. This is so bad that you've got to work a shovel under it, then pull and bang out all the dirt, throwing all the grass and roots into a wheelbarrow. If you leave any roots, the grass is back and must be re-pulled.

In one bed, I pulled all the grass and then scattered some California poppies and toadflax seeds in, figuring they would crowd out any grass or weeds. It worked beautifully and they'll reseed for next year, although they won't be so thick.

I love my little cheapo plastic fish pond! David and I planted it this spring, and now I have creeping lamium, pansies, violas, and Japanese iris around it. They make it look less plastic and more natural. We just caught the five goldfish I bought this spring to look pretty and keep down the mosquitoes. Here, the ice gets too thick for the fish to survive outside, so we will winter them in our big aquariums in the house. They've been in for two weeks and seem to have adjusted.

Getting ready for winter

My tomatoes did fairly well this summer, but were slow because of the heat and drought. When our fall frosts came, we picked every darned tomato in the garden and brought them in the house to ripen in the new greenhouse. They ripen faster when it's warm, and it was just too cold to risk them staying outside. Frost is one thing, but a bad freeze is another—it'll kill them to mush.

As the tomatoes ripen, I've been making tomato sauce, salsa, spaghetti sauce, and chili (for convenience and to use up some of my older dry beans). I still, at this November 1st writing, have baskets of tomatoes in all stages of ripe around the house. I've learned not to put tomatoes in a sunny window to ripen; they usually rot instead. Instead, I just put them in boxes and baskets and keep sorting them by ripeness. You lose a few to rot, but most of them ripen nicely with no muss and fuss.

My chicken coop not only was not very warm, but it looked like hell. I made it out of scraps of used lumber and OSB, sort of like a patchwork quilt. I had lots of pieces of tongue and groove 2x6 lumber left over from the house, so one sunny day, I set about tacking them to my coop, over the OSB. It turned out to look pretty nice, kind of like a log building. I also used up leftover insulation board and some old paneling Tom gave me to finish the inside. Now the coop is sturdier, warmer, and definitely looks nicer. I even built a flower box under the front window so the chickens can have their own flowers. No wonder my hens are singing.

I just found another pile of 2x6 pieces up by the travel trailer. Just what I need to finish off the front of the new pheasant pen we're building on the other side of the goat barn.

It's getting colder now and we're starting to cut and split wood in earnest. I want to split a couple of truck loads and stack them on the new enclosed porch. That way it'll be out of the rain, snow, and bad weather, nice and dry. And I'll only have to open the greenhouse door, go out on the dry porch and bring in wood to fill the wood box. Maybe ten steps in all. I can live with that.

I've been cleaning out the goat pen and donkey stall, hauling trailer loads of that old manure down onto

Me putting my new siding on the chicken coop

the garden where the corn will go next year. Corn is a very heavy feeder, liking the nitrogen that would cause problems with other crops. I'm also fertilizing those spots I had trouble with this summer. Hopefully I'll get it all well worked in by freeze-up. I didn't make it over the whole garden last fall, and boy was I sorry in the spring. So I'm trying to get it done soon. It won't be long until our freeze-up now. The geese landed on ice this morning. That's how it is in the northern backwoods; you do what you can, but never have it all done before winter hits. And you just learn to live with it and not take life too seriously. ✺

195

About the Author

In her own words, Jackie has lived a self-reliant lifestyle for "forty-something years," and plans to do it for the rest of her life. Jackie started writing for *Backwoods Home Magazine* in 1995 and her long-running advice column, *Ask Jackie*, is one of the most popular features in the magazine and on the *BHM* website, www.backwoodshome.com.

Jackie is a prolific writer who has written scores of articles on self-reliant living for *Backwoods Home Magazine*. She is also a trained field veterinary technician and coauthored the book, *Veterinary Guide for Animal Owners* with C.E. Spaulding. Her new, full-length book about growing and preserving all types of food and raising animals will be published in 2009 by *BHM*.

Jackie has developed homesteads in New Mexico, Montana, Michigan, and now lives in the woods of northern Minnesota with her mother and her son where she is building her newest homestead. *BHM's* ongoing feature, *Starting Over*, which began in the November/December 2004 issue, has chronicled the building of her northern Minnesota homestead where she continues to garden, preserve the harvest, tend her animals, and be self-reliant in every way.